Raising Responsible Teenagers

This book is a thank you to the hundreds of parents, young people and children who shared their experiences with me. Thanks also to my own children for not giving me any practice at managing difficult behaviour, and to my wife for her support.

All of these people have taught me the one thing that really matters: love (charity) does begin at home.

Raising Responsible Teenagers

Bob Myers

Jessica Kingsley Publishers
London

Designed and typeset by Alice Graphics
Line drawings by Peter Dodds
Edited by Mignon Turpin
Cover illustration by Peter Dodds

First published in 1996 in Australia by
The Australian Council for Educational Research Ltd,
Radford House, Frederick Street,
Hawthorn, Victoria 3122, Australia

First published in the United Kingdom in 1997 by
Jessica Kingsley Publishers Ltd
116 Pentonville Road
London N1 9JB, England

British Library Cataloguing in Publication Data
Myers, Bob, 1936-
Raising responsible teenagers / Bob Myers.
p.   cm.
Includes index.
ISBN 1-85302-429-5 (pbk. : alk. paper)
1. Parent and teenager. 2. Parenting. 3. Adolescence.
4. Responsibility in adolescence. I. Title.
HQ799,15.M94   1996
649'.125--dc20   96-34242
                                                            CIP

Printed and Bound in Great Britain by
Biddles Ltd., Guildford and King's Lynn

Contents

Introduction

PARENTING NOW AND IN the future is and will be very difficult. Parents are under pressure from all quarters to discipline children in a way that is acceptable within our society, where children have many of the rights of adults.

Parents become parents without any training and sometimes without much warning. Some are trying to do the job of raising children without knowing anything about child development and very little about how to deal with difficult behaviour.

By tackling three main areas – child development, parenting style and discipline – this book tries to fill these gaps by helping parents understand the complex issues involved in child development and by helping parents to help children gain the self-control needed to become competent adults.

Every topic in child development and discipline seems to go around in circles or be so dependent one on another that it is impossible to cover all

"YOU'RE LUCKY—MINE ARE STILL ON THEIR 'L' PLATES ! "

possibilities when talking about human behaviour. Generalities are unavoidable in order to make explanations simple enough to be interesting and readable. I make no apologies for making written discussion on this difficult subject as readable as I can.

Chapters 1, 2 and 4 explain the difficult subject of child personality, psychological, emotional and moral development, using everyday language, to give parents the background knowledge they need to understand the behaviour of their children and help them to realise that much of what parents see as unusual behaviour is quite normal.

The age from birth to four is fascinating and so important to the development of the child. So also is the period from then to the onset of adolescence, and no less so during adolescence. It is hoped that the chapters on child development, which were influenced by the works of James Fowler, will give the reader some sense of this fascinating time and a new way of looking at the problems of the teenage years.

Much of the behaviour of children appears to be blamed on the 'parenting style' used by the parent in their general treatment of the kids. The parenting style is blamed for everything from the outlook of the child to their way of working out problems. The subject of the parenting style used is mainly dealt with in Chapter 5 but there are many references to it scattered throughout the book. This is necessary because the parenting style used is so much a part of so many things that it is difficult to keep it separate, especially when it comes to topics like negotiating rules and consequences with children.

Three parenting styles – dominant, smothering and permissive – are discussed and coupled with three discipline methods – intervention, interaction and non-intervention – to show how they would apply in an ideal world and in the real world. However, the assertive negotiation of how things are to be done is important for the discipline of children of all ages and especially important again at adolescence. Chapters 6 and 7 look at the negotiation of boundaries, rules and limits that are causing problems within the home. Negotiation is only required on very few rules and this can be done using some specific guidelines discussed in these two chapters and in Chapter 4.

Chapter 8 looks at responsible behaviour and therefore at irresponsible behaviour with the emphasis on encouraging responsible behaviour or moving children away from a negative spiral of behaviour.

All parents are rightly interested in the discipline of children and how this can be done without violating the rights of children. Chapter 3 and Chapters 9 to 14 discuss this subject in many ways. Punishment is dealt with in detail and compared with logical and social consequences in handling difficult behaviour.

Practical examples from the experiences of many parents are given in Chapter 14 along with examples of placing the responsibility for the behaviour of the children where it belongs – with the children.

Sometimes adolescent behaviour can lead to relationships becoming so strained that the child may have to leave the family home, sometimes with a restraining order being necessary, but the last three chapters attempt to avoid this situation arising.

The final chapter argues that the parenting of children has become a community responsibility and parents need the support of the community, not criticism and blame, in countering the influences that come right into the modern home and those from well-intentioned people in the community whose actions can undermine the family.

CHAPTER 1

Child Development in the Early Years

PARTS OF THIS BOOK may upset you. Parts of it may strike at your basic values and beliefs but I don't know which parts will do that so I can't leave them out. Anyway, I don't want to leave them out because the whole idea of the book is to increase your knowledge about parenting. Knowledge is power and parents need an injection of power in their parenting in order to cope with the challenge of parenting.

The pressures on parents have changed over the past few years and many of the methods used by parents in the past are no longer acceptable. Unfortunately there has been very little done to give parents another way of coping with the special problems facing today's parents.

In the early 1980s there was a concerted effort made to prepare school administrations and teachers for the change away from the use of corporal punishment and other punitive means of disciplining children. Many schools and individual teachers resisted the change (some still do) but the changes came in and along with those came the education of the children about their rights.

The unfortunate part of all this isn't that the changes came and it isn't because the children were taught their rights (they should know them) but that parents were neglected in all this. A situation developed where some people, such as teachers and children, had been given knowledge that others, parents, had not been given. Knowledge is power so in effect the parents had been disempowered and could easily be used as scapegoats to blame for the behaviour of the kids.

At times you may think I'm doing my own bit of parent-bashing but it is in the context of being realistic enough to acknowledge that some parents are sadistic brutes who should never be allowed to parent children. I also realise that there are parents who will misuse the increased power that knowledge brings, just as they misuse their present power.

For the vast majority of parents, however, the power gained will be used to increase their power over their parenting rather than their power over their children.

Throughout the book I will alternate the use of 'him' and 'her' rather than constantly saying 'him/her' or 'she/he' and, because my definition of a child is any person under the age of 17, I will use the terms child, teenager, young person, kids, adolescents rather freely because that is the way people talk, and to impress that a teenager is still a child needing guidance.

My first task is to give some background knowledge of the very complicated and complex subject of child development in regard to psychological, emotional, moral, social and general personality. I am not a psychologist or a psychiatrist so what I present is a layman's view of these very complex issues. I believe that my greatest advantage in explaining these theories is that I am a person who has worked closely with children for over twenty-two years and have a keen interest in their development.

Before we start I want to make one thing clear. A danger in learning about child development is that you may get the idea that it is too late to do anything about any damage that has occurred in the past and any feelings of failure you already have will be made worse. I don't believe it is ever too late and you certainly can't start any earlier than now to correct problems from the past. The second point is that you may have made mistakes and you may have been mistaken but you no doubt did what you believed was right at the time. What more can you do? Anyone who expects more is unreasonable.

Infancy

The basic personality of a child is formed in the first two years of life. Part of that personality starts to form even as the parents are still feeling the first frights and awe of becoming parents.

During the first 18 months the baby will gain a sense that the people in her world can generally be trusted to meet her needs, if she has been lucky enough to be born into such a family, or she will get the sense that people generally cannot be trusted to meet her needs. Before she became aware of people she just had this feeling, or sense, of the environment being trustworthy or untrustworthy in meeting her needs.

Now, let's get something clear. I am not trying to tell you that the baby thinks, 'Oh, I have been born into a very untrustworthy environment'. No, it is just a sense, a feeling that all is well or all is not well. There is no actual thought.

There is a gnawing feeling (hunger) that magically gets relieved as pleasant sounds and touchings go on. There is a feeling of discomfort (soiled nappy) that is also relieved by the same shape that appeared when the gnawing was fixed up. This same shape is where the pleasant sounds, smell and touch come from and that shape usually comes quickly and feels good.

After a while the baby is able to distinguish that shape from other similar shapes that don't have the same smell, feel or sound. That is the other achievement of babies in the first 18 months, being able to distinguish between shapes and start to realise that when a person (shape, object) moves out of sight it doesn't mean it is gone forever. The baby can have faith that when mother leaves the room she still exists and will return. How does she learn this?

One way is through the seemingly silly game of 'Peek-a-boo'. Mother disappears and reappears, disappears and reappears, accompanied by laughter and smiles. Mother leaving the room can then leave a feeling of anticipation of her

return. Attachment grows but at the same time a faith in allowing the object of that attachment to leave her sight. It is easy to see how theorists couple this stage with the beginnings of faith and hope. It is also easy to see how this trust can become distrust when neglect occurs.

Okay, so now you reckon all you have to do is satisfy the every need and wish of the baby to give her a deep feeling of trust and faith. Is that really desirable? A healthy level of distrust is necessary in a dangerous world where there are people who will do the child harm. What is a healthy level of trust and how do you gauge the amount the baby is getting? It's easy to weigh her to see how much milk she is getting but impossible to test how much trust she is absorbing. This will come out in her behaviour later and give the parent a chance to make adjustments.

In other words, a baby gets a basic level of trust or distrust of the world, and of people, starting in the very first contact with the world and so the first bit is put in place in building a personality. She has also started on the first part of psychological development by being able to distinguish objects. In addition, she has started her own way of deciding values for herself in the only way she knows how, by sticking them in her mouth to test for taste or the relief of teething pains.

The level of trust that results from this first stage can be built on or eroded in later stages so there is always hope if you want to lift a child's level of trust. However, there is also the problem that if the child is over-indulged, she may develop the idea that she is to have every wish granted when she wants it granted and will continue to demand to have her wishes granted regardless of the needs of others.

What I want you to understand is that for every stage we are going to be talking about there is a good thing to be gained for the personality of the child. The problem is that it is impossible to know how much of the good thing the child is getting until later on when her behaviour will give some indication. That is when the parent can try to make adjustments through the discipline methods used.

So you be the judge of how much cuddling and playing you want to do with your child and take no notice of people who tell you, 'You will spoil her if you nurse her so much'. How much is too much? There can never be too much love but love sometimes means letting a baby cry to learn to cope with some discomfort until the trusted one is ready to give attention.

The baby is now off and running on the lifelong job of making sense of the world and what sense she makes of it will be seen in the way she acts. She will learn from the world, she will be shaped by the world and she will shape her world.

The independent 2-to-3-year-old

As the child moves to the ripe old age of two he has become so good at seeing the difference between objects that he is now aware that he can be separate to others and starts to explore his growing ability to do things for himself. The 2-year-old has hit the scene with his exaggerated sense of his own ability to be independent and quickly finds that there is a need to learn the beginnings of self-control.

Besides self-control there are other tasks to achieve at this age, not the least of which is to learn the language. This is an enormous task that he does with amazing speed. In the beginning he just learns single words like 'No', 'Me' and 'Mine' that go along with the rebellious tendency and quickly learns to put two words together like, 'Me do' to further express that independence.

When this independence is firmly but gently handled the child will have a sense of autonomy added to his personality. A sense of being able to stand on his own two feet with the approval of the people he trusts. However, he may get more of the opposite, a sense of shame and doubt if his efforts are belittled and punished.

Personality theories place a lot of importance on another task of this age; toilet training. It's easy enough to laugh at this but again we have to look at it without thinking of the child as deliberately acting out what the theories say. Try to look at it from the child's point of view. The task at this age is to undergo toilet training while trying to make sense of being praised for doing something that feels so good coming out but which suddenly and magically becomes 'Yuk' if he goes to play with it.

Parents make such a fuss about his success or failure on the potty that it becomes the focus of the child's attention and therefore influences how he makes sense of everything that is happening around him. Sometimes praise comes when the good stuff is given to the potty quickly and sometimes holding on is praised. It could then become part of the personality of the young child that giving is good (generosity) or that holding back is good (meanness).

If this is right then it is at this stage that the beginning of the personality trait of co-operation and sharing appears. It is also possible that the giving or holding on could become part of the self-control, or rebellion part of the two year old's daily life. The very beginnings of power struggle relationships could start at this age between parent and child or between the child and his world in general. The child may come to have a sense of being in a win/lose world where he gets his own way by fighting for it or he may learn to manipulate his own way by appearing helpless.

What an important age this is shaping up to be. But remember that 'a sense of' does not mean that whatever level of autonomy is formed at this age is set for life. It can be altered at later stages but the sooner the better and the sooner the easier.

A sense of being 'my own boss' is one end of the scale of the elements added to the personality around this age. At the other end of the scale is the sense of shame, of being a worthless thing.

The sense of shame can come about because of the 2-year-old becoming aware of himself as a separate person. Being aware of himself means being self-conscious and when we are self-conscious we believe everyone is looking at us. We feel exposed and tend to judge ourselves harshly.

Maybe a little shame is good to keep us humble but the 2-year-old will judge himself so harshly that he doesn't need any shaming by us. What he needs is a great deal of gentle but firm guidance that doesn't give in to his tantrums and manipulative behaviour. This is the time for him to learn that there is a right and a wrong way to get what he wants.

The feeling of shame is not the beginning of a conscience or the beginning of moral behaviour because a sense of guilt has to come from the child having wronged someone or something outside of the child. The child at this stage is extremely self-centred so the sense of shame is an inward sense of self-value that may come from, and have a great effect on, a child's toilet performance and general behaviour at age two to three (and onwards to age eighty-two).

I mentioned at the start of this section that the 2-year-old has become good at seeing the differences in objects. A little story may serve to illustrate how important this can be in everyday life for the child and how the parent can become aware of the development of the child in other areas.

One day my 2-year-old grand-daughter picked up a linen handkerchief from the floor. It was just a plain square except for a maroon border. She declared, 'Nanna's!' and went off to give it to Nanna. Being curious about these things, I waited about ten minutes and then, holding it up by the corners, showed her another plain linen handkerchief with a maroon border, one of mine. 'Who does this belong to Heidi?' Without hesitation she declared in a definite tone, 'Poppy'.

So what's the big deal? The big deal is that she was apparently using the relative sizes of objects to judge something else, in this case who owned the object. The other part of the big deal is that she had shown a sign of being aware even at that age of differences in what is appropriate for a male thing and what is appropriate for a female. A sign that the child's sex role training begins very early.

As if all that isn't enough, we have another extremely important thing happening early in this stage. The child is becoming a mimic. She copies everything as she watches closely and unfortunately copies the bad with the good. This is the beginning of taking in the values of the parents. If parents want to learn something about themselves, and what other people notice about them, they only have to watch and listen to their small children.

Even from this brief discussion about 2-year-olds it becomes obvious why this stage is seen as being so important in the development of a child. However, once again it is impossible to know how much autonomy the child is getting from this stage to mix with the level of trust that was brought along from the previous stage. A perfect parent would know but the perfect parent doesn't exist.

One thing I am very sure of is that little kids should never be shamed as a way of trying to develop their conscience, or for any other reason. Shaming a child is likely to have the opposite effect, that of developing the sense that it is alright to get away with it if no-one is looking, or, if there is too much heaped on her, she may develop 'shamelessness' as a defence.

The preschooler: 3-to-6-year-old

She has gained a level of self-control, has lost some of the persistence or obsessiveness that was so frustrating in the 2-year-old and now has a good grasp of the language.

In the early part of this stage there are times when you wish she didn't have such a grasp of the use of 'Why'. This does pass but the quest for a reason is a strong part of this stage. What she will gain for her personality here is the sense of there being a purpose to behaviour, to develop her 'get up and go', her sense of initiative, her desire to start something happening.

She will also continue to form a strong sense of her sex role, how she should act as a female. Times are changing but for most at this stage the old ways still apply and girls are taught to be passive and attractive to get what they want while boys are encouraged to be aggressive and 'go get em'.

The other end of the scale for this stage is that she is very aware of rules. Rules about sex role, rules within and about the language, rules in the house (don't do this, don't do that), rules of the games she plays. In fact this stage is very much about law and order things and about sounds of praise or condemnation.

The main caregivers will be the main teachers and models for kids of this age as they watch the example of adults and start to pick up values and a sense of whether the power of life comes from material or spiritual things. In the past, the main caregivers at this stage were the parents and extended family but this is increasingly being done by substitute caregivers, in day-care centres and kindergartens, as both parents work. In some cases this is good because the level of care can be much higher than it is in the home.

By now the child has developed a very limited ability to see things from another person's point of view. I was walking to school with young Kyle, 5, and he asked very earnestly, 'Hey Pop, you know ants?' (He always starts that way and I always have to say 'yes' before he will go on.) 'Yes, I know ants'. He went on, 'Whenever it rains, they have a flood'. A little further along he says, 'Hey Pop, you know ants?' 'Yes, I know ants'. 'To ants, the grass is like trees'. This is profound stuff at that time of the morning and it shows he has the beginnings of being able to see things from another point of view. However, any attempt to keep the conversation going resulted in him going 'off with the fairies' as he dropped back into the usual 5-year-old's interests and way of thinking.

Kids at this stage can come up with real gems of wisdom that leave an adult thinking they must be really mature. The gems are normal and so is the drop back to fantasy. The basis for wisdom is there but it can't be sustained because imagination is a dominant part of this age.

Being aware of rules and having some ability to see another person's point of view sets the stage for the sounds of condemnation to bring the beginnings of a sense of guilt. Unlike shame, which is directed on the self, now we have the beginnings of a feeling of responsibility towards someone or something else and this is what is necessary for the development of conscience. However, at this age the size of the wrongdoing is judged by the amount of reaction she gets to what was done. A very loud response means the act was worse than an act that gets a quiet response.

Making a big mess by accident is worse than deliberately making a small mess. The intention behind what was done is not part of her way of judging right and wrong at this stage.

Sibling rivalry is another feature of this age (if there are any other kids in the family). Things have changed from the child being the centre of attention without much effort, to the child having to compete with others for the attention of the mother. Much of the purpose of behaviour is aimed towards finding a place in the family, using initiative to find ways of occupying the time of the mother.

As with the other parts of the personality, the child doesn't sit and think of ways of solving the problem of how to keep the mother's attention. The rivalry behaviour is a response to one of the strongest of human needs: the need to belong. Up until the child became really aware of herself as being a separate person, the need to belong wasn't a problem but now it becomes a strong motivation for her behaviour.

Just as the 'terrible twos' can see the start of power struggle problems, this stage can see the start of what is known as attention seeking. What form this will take must depend on the amount of will and persistence left from the previous stage; if there are siblings the competition for attention may become extreme.

Cartoons, fairy tales, television and religion introduces the child at this age to the incomprehensible but instinctively frightening thing called 'death' and I wonder what the child's imagination does with this concept. Certainly there is a need for a certain amount of fear of death and injury so she develops a healthy respect for dangerous situations and objects.

So, incredible as it may seem, before the child leaves the preschool stage the personality has its complete base. The psychological and moral base is in place and so is the value/power base. From now on it is a matter of 'which of the components of these things will be developed and which will be damaged as the child grows?'

Many of the problems the child has overcome up to now will surface again at adolescence and the same love, attention, patience and firm guidance that got her through this first era of her life will also get her through at adolescence.

However, there is a long way to go before adolescence and life along the way will set the stage for whether the emergence of adolescence is explosive or smooth.

The child entering the next stage with a healthy level of trust may be in for a rude shock and have that trust destroyed or it may be strengthened. A child with a low sense of self-worth may be lucky enough to have someone notice and have the self-esteem boosted, or it may be further weakened by being ridiculed.

The parents also have their own life problems. Family circumstances can change. Maybe the family will stay together, maybe not. Divorce, separation, taking up with a violent new partner, movement to a new town, financial problems. All of these things affect the parents and distract them from the problems of the kids.

All that we can be sure of is that the mix of trust, autonomy, initiative and all the things that go with them will change as the child grows and is influenced by all sorts of things. Usually the parent will be the main influence but feeling guilty about something going wrong is not justified because the parent will be totally unaware of the existence of so many of the influences on a child.

Sufficient to say that the child's behaviour will always be the expression of values and beliefs the child is picking up from her interpretation of the world around her. In later chapters we will look at things you can do about altering that behaviour and when I believe a parent can be 'blamed' for a child's bad behaviour.

Childhood: the 6-to-12-year-old

The main task for the child moving into and through this stage is to separate what is real from what appears to be real. The child is entering the age of reason. You may ask, 'Why do they call it the age of reason?'

According to the idea of there being definite stages of development, a transformation occurs in the child's thinking at this stage. The idea is that she is always trying to make sense of the world and as long as what she sees and hears can be fitted in with the way she now thinks, nothing much changes in the way she thinks. There is no need for any change.

However, if more and more happens that the child strives to understand but can't, the amount of unexplained information forces the brain to develop a way of sorting out the mess. The development that is forced to occur around age six or seven is the ability to use logical thinking, to sort things out in sequence and to see that there is a definite connection between what happened and what caused it to happen. Another advance is that she becomes aware that what is done can be undone, things can be reversed.

A simple example of this is now being able to cope with learning to add and to reverse this by subtraction. To multiply and reverse it by dividing. To plan something on paper and then make it. The child learns to have control of things and can alter the outcome by altering what she does.

She becomes more settled and less boisterous, more sure of what to do and how to do it. She quickly learns about tools and how to use them. Those tools can be anything at all: hammers, problem solving, words, clothes, interpersonal skills, in fact anything needed to help cope with the environment.

Another big development is that the child can tell stories in great detail and can make up stories. However, she cannot see the overall meaning of the story, what is called 'the moral of the story'.

Because this stage is tied up so much in doing things and in the use of tools, the addition to the personality will be a sense of competence. The opposite end of this scale is inferiority.

Again it is very difficult to know the amount of competence gained because kids become so good at hiding feelings of inferiority by appearing over-confident. The jug that pours confidence into a child is labelled 'Encouragement and Respect' and the one that pours inferiority in is labelled 'Ridicule and Lack of Opportunity'.

What track does the moral development take? This is the time that he needs to see the value in rules and keeping to rules, otherwise he cannot move to the next stage of moral development. Between six and twelve is when the awareness of rules that came about in the previous stage becomes more dominant. All sorts of things are taken up that require rules to give the activities meaning and safety for the participant.

Board games are learned, team games, house rules, club rules, school rules, street rules, shop rules, all sorts of rules in all sorts of settings. Children of this age can become very strict on sticking to rules and see wrongdoing as being the breaking of rules rather than the effects of that action on people.

The child becomes good at making up rules to solve problems that come up because fairness and justice are very important to her, even though the fairness is still seen very much from the child's own point of view. What is seen as fair may be what gives her an advantage.

There is also the opposite; if there wasn't enough will power gained (too much shame) from the 2-year-old stage then he may constantly give the advantage to the other kids. Another possibility from the same cause is that he may begin to see the rules as something only to keep to when someone is watching, and may believe it is the responsibility of other people to keep him to the rules. Jails are full of people who grow up believing this and blaming other people.

" *BECAUSE GIRLS WITH PLAITS NEVER HAVE FIRST RIDE... & THAT'S THE RULE !* "

Justice at this stage is on the basis of 'an eye for an eye, tooth for a tooth'. This can be taken literally or be seen in his reluctance to do anything without being paid, the 'what's in it for me?' response to requests to do something. A fair day's pay for a fair day's work.

By now values have been acquired from many sources. Some are good, some are bad, some will be a mystery as to where they came from. Along with a general education, school has been a tremendous influence on this value system as she has learnt to cope with a whole social system with its many dangers. Not the least of which is schoolyard violence.

God will be seen as being a human figure, most likely male, who gives out justice in rewards or punishments. Religious symbols may be confused with, and be as sacred as, what they represent.

Heading into adolescence

From here on this explanation of child development can get very complicated because there are so many possibilities for how a child develops. I have chosen four lines to follow which so far have kept more or less together but now those lines may take off in different directions. There is an added complication in that three of the lines may not keep up with the fourth or with each other.

The four lines are: *personality, logical thinking, moral judgement,* and *the value/power base.*

The personality line is also the age line and will keep going regardless of what the others do and each child will have to deal with all of the problems that come along at each age. However, the development of logical thinking, of moral judgement, and of the value and power base may go ahead at different speeds to each other or any one or all of them may not develop past this stage.

Some kids will go into the next stage of logical thinking at age 11, some at 15, some at 20, some never. The same can be said for the moral judgement and the value/power base. The development of the moral judgement and the value/power base cannot go ahead if logical thinking doesn't go ahead but logical thinking can go ahead even if the moral judgement and/or the value/power base don't go ahead. I did say it was going to get complicated!

None of this in itself makes for better or worse kids but certainly it affects how each of them will go about solving their problems and accounts for the incredible variety of opinions and ways of living. Each child has their own unique combination of the four lines we are following and within those four lines is a unique combination of what they have got out of each stage of their lives so far. The possible combinations are endless.

Before we consider adolescence I want to add something to what was said earlier about how development occurs in logical thinking. I said then that children are always trying to make sense of the world, to find meaning, and that development to the next stage occurs when their present way of thinking can no longer make sense of what they see, hear, feel, taste and smell.

Stimulation is what I am talking about. New things to sense, new things to try and make sense of and find how they fit into the puzzle of the world. New puzzles in everyday life that don't fit into the present way of thinking.

What is true for logical thinking is also true for the development of moral judgement and the value/power base. Being faced with puzzles, dilemmas, other ways of looking at things that stimulate a new way of thinking, a way that is unique to each person.

Things to think about

✔ For every stage of a child's development there is a good thing to be gained for the personality of the child.

✔ Basic trust or distrust is born in infancy.

✔ Self-control, independence, co-operation and sharing begin in the 2-to-3-year-old stage.

✔ Children of preschooler age become aware of themselves as being separate people and so their need to belong, to find their place in the family, is strong.

✔ Competence, the ability to use logical thinking, and an increased awareness of rules develops when the child is 6-to-12-years-old.

✔ Stimulation is essential for a child to move from one stage to the next.

✔ It is never too late to correct problems from the past and you can't start any earlier than now.

CHAPTER 2

Development During Adolescence

Stages of adolescence

ADOLESCENCE IS GENERALLY treated as being one stage of life that extends from around 13 to 21 for girls and around 14 to 24 for boys. However, adolescence is such a complicated and difficult time to describe that I am going to divide it into two parts. I will call these parts Stage One and Stage Two adolescence.

Even in doing this I will have to give only a general overview of the whole picture. As I said in Chapter 1 the possible combinations of *personality, logical thinking, moral judgement* and *the value/power base* are endless.

I will take stage one adolescence as being the period of overlap of actual adolescence and the previous stage the value/power base and stage two adolescence as being a 'normal' combination of age-related physical development which assumes that logical thinking, moral judgement and value/power base development has kept up to some extent.

Although I divide adolescence into two parts, many kids go through the first part very quickly, to the extent that it doesn't seem to exist. Others take some time to pass from what I call stage one adolescence to stage two adolescence and others never develop past stage one adolescence, except physically.

What I am calling stage one adolescence could be thought of as describing the turmoil time between two stages. The time where what the child is seeing, hearing, feeling, tasting and smelling doesn't make much sense and the child is trying to understand life using the thinking from the previous stage. If he manages to make sense of what's happening by using the logic he knows so well, there will be no need to develop the next stage in logical thinking.

Briefly put, the deep need to make sense of the world will force the change in thinking if there is sufficient and appropriate stimulation. This happens because sense cannot be made of his new world by using the thinking from the previous stage.

Obviously, for parents who want to have a high influence on what that stimulation is and therefore on the outcome of this stage, adolescence is a time for careful and controlled parenting, not for arguing and fighting.

There are many big tasks for the adolescent to cope with, not the least of which comes from the body changes that bring about all sorts of tensions from inside and outside of that body. Stirrings of independence and hearing so many opinions of other people that don't fit in with those that have been learned can leave feelings of confusion and fear.

Developing physically earlier or later than friends of the same age can add a further burden to an already heavy load of tasks and problems.

They may also have to cope with the added tensions caused by the parents being into their late 30s, with their own tensions and life changes. The trend towards having children later in life adds to the so called generation gap.

Every adolescent is unique so I am forced to generalise about adolescents. Every person is extremely complex so I am forced to simplify the explanation to make any sense at all. For this chapter I am going to deal separately

" CHRIS SAYS HE OFTEN FEELS THAT HE DOESN'T FIT IN... "

with each of the four lines we have been following so that I can show the difference between the two stages of adolescence within that part of a person's development.

Personality

When a person moves from childhood into early adolescence he has a level of self-esteem and skills gained during the long period of 'childhood'. This means that he may have a good feeling about himself and a sense of importance and competence to solve problems, or may feel inferior and useless. The child may feel unable to do much, doesn't know much and is not very important.

Whatever the level of competence and self-esteem of the young person moving into adolescence, that level will either increase or decrease over the adolescent period, depending on the encouragement or put downs encountered as the child tries to cope with the enormous changes that are occurring in and around him.

The main task during adolescence is to solve the same type of problem he had to solve early in life but this time it is on a much bigger scale. Back then he became aware of himself as being a separate member of a family group and had to work out his place in that group. This led to the sibling rivalry for the attention of the parent.

The adolescent has become aware of himself as being a separate individual in a society, a person who has to work out who he is and where he fits in to that social set-up. The young person becomes very aware of being an individual who acts very differently depending on which group he is with at the time.

What the young person will be left with as part of the personality at the end of adolescence is the sense of being a person who can move easily between the role played as a member of the society, as a member of different groups within that society, with individuals, and with one special individual.

The other end of the scale is the great feeling of loneliness that the awareness of being separate can bring. Moving from role to role can lead to complete confusion, especially if faced with two of those roles at the same time. For example, a meeting of his mother and his friends can lead to feeling torn as to which role to play, the son or the friend. This can be a real problem if the young person doesn't have a 'me' who can bridge the gap.

Stage two adolescents are very self-conscious and I read somewhere that they use people like mirrors that reflect how they appear to other people, to help them develop their identity. But just imagine how hard it would be to figure out what you really look like by wandering through a fun parlour of distorted mirrors. The adolescent's task is to put these distorted images together to form a person who has the self-confidence to face whatever the future holds. People who are being used as mirrors for a young person should be aware of the importance of the image they are showing to the young person.

In other words, solving the so called identity crisis can lead to 'getting himself together', forming a strong identity and thus becoming a person who knows who he is and where he is going. If the adolescent doesn't get his identity 'together', he will be confused about who he is, this person who seems to be different persons at different times, and his day-to-day self-esteem will be dictated by the actions of others as he goes through life.

One 16-year-old-girl told me it was as if other people were like newspapers and she was cutting bits off every one she met and pasting them on herself to make up who she was. She was a bit of every one she met. A 14-year-old boy expressed surprise at the realisation that other people also had a 'life inside their head'.

Sexual identity is a major part of the identity crisis and is a difficult one because of the unfamiliar feelings towards other people of both sexes. Until this is sorted out the adolescent can be confused as to whether they are 'friend feelings' or 'sex partner feelings'. This confusion can be increased by the fantasies played out in the adolescent's mind; fantasies that can lead to having doubts about both sexuality and sanity. For a boy especially, these fantasies can take up a large part of his mental life as he develops to his sexual peak around age 15 and tries to find ways to satisfy his urges. (The doubts about sanity may well be why so many adolescents get upset at any suggestion of seeing a psychologist or psychiatrist.)

The feeling of being 'different' is what leads a young person to believe that he must have been adopted. He has strong feelings of being different to the other members of the family. This feeling is not to be laughed at but it can seem amusing when this replica of his father is claiming to have been adopted.

Feeling different can and does lead to feeling very alone, as if no-one knows him, no-one will listen, no-one thinks he is important. Again this feeling should be treated with respect and taken seriously because the feeling of being isolated from others may become part of the personality. The feeling of being isolated is also a major factor in suicide.

The feeling of isolation can be heightened if sibling rivalry has been strong within the family because now there is the equivalent in the new crisis. Rivalry with other members of the society, and even with her own friends, for jobs, status, and relationships.

Her basic way of solving problems will be aggressive, submissive or cooperative. This may be because of how she has been treated and the example she has been given, or it may be a temporary defence from the uncertainty of unfamiliar thoughts and feelings.

This leads us to the single most distinguishing thing about adolescence: it is a deeply emotional time, especially in the early part of stage two adolescence. The release of hormones result in deeply felt emotions that influence, and often control, the behaviour of the teenager. Added to this is a heightened self-awareness and a very delicate self-esteem. If we can keep all this in mind we may find it easier to understand the difficulties faced by the adolescent, and the parents. The sudden mood changes and flare ups, the very fast changes in who is the 'love of his life'.

School work may take second place to the social life at school and trying to get them to do homework becomes a constant battle. Some adolescents only do enough work to keep the teacher off their back while they get on with the important things of life, like making friends and planning their night life. They spend all night on the phone talking to the people they have been with all day.

School achievement becomes very serious for some and all their effort is put into getting high marks for the all-important final year so they can get into university. To fail at this is to fail as a person.

Logic

The stage one adolescent may have set ideas on how things should be done and believe there is only one right way to do things. Add this to his mastery of logic and you can see why he can become a real bush lawyer in arguing endlessly in support of one view of life.

"WELL .. WHY I SHOULD BE ALLOWED TO BORROW THE CAR TO DRIVE MY FRIENDS TO THE ROCK FESTIVAL ALL SEEMS PERFECTLY LOGICAL TO ME ! "

In this stage the young person thinks mainly in regard to the immediate past and the present and therefore is unlikely to look far into the past or want to make provision for the future. This is seen in the way he seems to think only about what is wanted now, things have to happen NOW and he can't bear to wait. 'Wait' is a 'dirty word' to a young teenager.

Considering consequences is not a big part of stage one thinking because the future is seen as being little different to the present, the way the world is now is the way it will always be, and he finds it hard or impossible to see how the past has affected the present or how the present will affect the future.

This changes in stage two adolescence because the young person becomes able to use what is called the 'scientific method' of solving problems. This means being able to see that there may be many different ways to solve a problem, that a change to any one of the many parts of a situation can cause a different outcome. The young person can see that introducing something new to a situation can change the outcome. Maths is a good example of this; in his school work the teenager is now more able to understand how changing and rearranging any of the numbers in an equation can change the answer.

This can be seen in everyday life in him now having the ability to see the bigger picture, how the past has affected the present and how decisions made now can affect the future. He can see that it is possible to change what happens by changing how things are done now. However, if his self-esteem is low he may be afraid to change behaviour for fear of being rejected or ridiculed.

When the stage one adolescent is asked about a movie on TV he will be able to give a detailed blow by blow description of the show but nothing about the 'theme' hidden in the story. The stage two adolescent can see the hidden theme of discrimination or race superiority or free love or whatever. (Whether a young person can do this is a way of deciding if she is mature enough to be watching 'Mature' videos.)

Another development for the stage two adolescent is the ability to think in the abstract and maths is again a good example of this, because now the adolescent is able to substitute letters for the numbers in an equation and it still makes sense.

In everyday life this abstract thinking may show up in the ability to have an ideal against which to judge people, behaviour and things and those ideals might be anything: the ideal mother, footballer, movie star, pop group, fashions, fads or religious concepts.

A common example of the stage two adolescent's ability to use abstract thinking is that he becomes quite the philosopher who can drive you crazy talking about things like, 'thinking about thinking' or about being able to 'think about how I think I think'. Or maybe he will talk about the universe and the meaning of life, and be taunting you with explanations for the meaning of life that are different to yours.

In earlier stages we have considered how the child has become aware of himself as being separate to other objects in the world and has gradually developed the ability to see things from the other person's point of view. At stage two adolescence there is a new development in this. Now he can see that there can be a difference in the judgement of what is seen. To show the changes I will give three examples, one from childhood, one from stage one adolescence and one from stage two adolescence.

At childhood Susie was asked how she would describe herself. 'Tall, red hair, freckles, good at tennis', she replied. When asked how her mother would describe her she replied, 'Tall, red hair, freckles, good at tennis'. There may be little or no difference in the descriptions because Susie had not developed the ability to see that people see her differently to how she sees herself.

At stage one adolescence Susie was again asked how she would describe herself. 'Good at basketball, helpful around the house, not very pretty, ugly hair', she replied. When asked how her mother would describe her she replied, 'Good at basketball, has an untidy room, nice hair, kind to animals'. There is a difference between the descriptions although they are still generally concrete things.

At stage two adolescence Susie was again asked to describe herself, 'I have lots of friends, know all the words of the top ten, am sick of boys and like dancing and music', she replied. When asked how her mother would describe her she replied, 'Pretty, friendly but can't hold friends, always bright and helpful but has an untidy room'. The difference here is that the description has changed to social and interpersonal words, with a difference between the descriptions.

Whether the young person has developed the new level of logical thinking typical of stage two adolescence will greatly affect the way she looks at life and values and the moral judgements made. If the child doesn't develop this ability, and there is no guarantee she will, it doesn't mean she is backward or a lesser person, it only means that problems will be solved in a different way.

Moral judgement

The stage one adolescent may be concerned with material things, with abilities and possessions, showing off and having little awareness of the feelings of others.

Stage one adolescents don't give much thought to people outside of those interacted with on a day-to-day basis and those very much relied on for external control of their behaviour. A major change in feelings from childhood to this in-between stage occurs here; the need for freedom rises and causes the dilemma that he still very much needs outside authority but may refuse to accept it from the parents. The breaking away process has begun.

Previously, childhood interests outside the family took up a lot of time as she joined group activities and learned a great deal about the advantages of teamwork and the importance of rules in teams. This may now take the form of peer group or maybe 'gang' membership which provides security because anyone who picks on a member has to account to the whole group. He will probably take up with friends and activities that are consistent with how the young person sees himself or would like to be, and those chosen friends can become the only important ones in life at the moment.

As part of the need for outside control, the stage one adolescent's general sense of right and wrong relies heavily on specific sets of rules, limits and firm guidance. However, because of the young person's need to show independence, these restrictions may not be accepted from the parents. These young people put a literal interpretation to rules and may insist on the parent producing fingerprints and photographs as evidence about any wrongdoing.

A curious thing happens at this stage. For a time many stage one adolescents who were very strict about sticking to rules start using the truth as a tool to get their own way. Lies become a part of living and rules are only kept to if there is a great chance of getting caught. They believe that the only time they get into trouble is when they get caught so the only thing they do wrong is to get caught. There is a lot of logic in that if it's looked at from a punishment perspective. Unfortunately some continue to think that way, but for most trust becomes important again as they move into stage two where the keeping of promises is so important.

Misbehaviour at stage one adolescence can become very similar to misbehaviour at very early childhood, like using a lot of toilet talk or obscene language, being messy in the toilet, or dropping their pants and 'flashing a browneye'. Some may revert to other infantile misbehaviour like throwing food around. Some typical stage one misbehaviour is defiance of time limits, having an untidy bedroom, ignoring jobs around the house, smoking, drinking and staying out all night.

They see parents as always doing what they think is best but have begun to see that parents are no longer always right and their way of doing things is not the only way it can be done.

For the stage one adolescent, justice is fairness but the fairness is judged mainly from their own point of view and this can result in an 'eye for an eye' and a 'tooth for a tooth'; there has to be payback for wrongs done to them and sometimes this can mean the use of weapons.

Parents tend to push for the child to be co-operative because kids should care about other people but it is doubtful that the early adolescent is capable of thinking like that. This would be quite normal because the child is very self-centred and the fact is that this self-centredness means co-operation at this stage is usually only important so he can get his own needs satisfied.

Stage two adolescents remain very self-conscious but now it is about how they should act in regard to the roles they see themselves playing. Being self-conscious means being self-centred, so that hasn't changed from stage one, but now they believe that actions are 'right' if they act according to how they think people who are important to them would expect them to act. How they think they will be judged as a surfie, or as a friend, or as a male/female, or as a son/daughter.

Like the early adolescent, at stage two they rely very much on outside authority for guidance but now it means sticking to peer group rules and the trends set by idols, even though they will claim that there was no pressure applied to them by anyone. They identify with these people and being near the people they identify with helps their feelings of belonging, so they want to spend all their time with the peer group. They become extremely emotionally involved with groups or individuals and tend to share everything with them. This new level of social moral reasoning may later develop into a true sense of responsibility towards others or it may always remain as a self-centred outlook on right and wrong, of 'what's in it for me?'

The stage two adolescent often experiences a strong confusion of loyalties in deciding how to act. Keeping promises and agreements becomes very important to them but when faced with the dilemma of having to choose between loyalty to two groups, such as family and friends, which group conformity will win? Or if the dilemma is between loyalty to the law at the expense of his own needs, will the individual needs win out?

The fact that they act so differently in different roles is just part of being a teenager. But this is no different to adults who 'play up' when they are away where no-one knows them. Teenagers, and many adults, identify with group rules but have not internalised those rules, they are rules that apply in that group and once they are away from the group they may act in an entirely different way.

A new role emerges at adolescence. The sex role has been relatively easy through childhood but now there are pressures coming from all directions telling them how to act. They are so conscious of doing what is right for each role played, and most roles have fairly clear rules, but this is not so for the sex role

There are double standards everywhere on this one. Television is warning about the dangers of AIDS and other sexually transmitted diseases but the movies and soapies have couples jumping into bed in the next scene after meeting and before they ask each other, 'What's your name?'

The adolescent's limited ability to see far into the future and the reliance on the people and things present 'now' for self-esteem may lead them into all sorts of dangerous activities, including very dangerous sexual activity. They don't want to seem different and 'weird'.

Although things are changing, females are still socialised to please males and are not taught about the implications of this when their efforts at finding their values and identity come into contact with the male at the peak of his sex drive. The peak for a female is much later in life and at adolescence she is more concerned with what the boys will think of her. Many adolescent girls confuse a boy's sex drive as being a commitment to her as a person.

The value/power base

I haven't said much about the value/power base. This is a difficult concept to explain because it underlies everything a person thinks and does. It is what we see as giving meaning to life, the sense that life is based on love or money or politics or religion or possessions or status or sport or fun, or a mixture of these.

Some would call it the 'attitude to life', others would call it a 'world outlook', others would call it 'faith'. Whatever 'it' is underlies all of a person's actions and thinking and is what people are trying to know when they talk about 'getting in touch with themselves'. It is the mixture of all the values we pick up along the journey of life folded into, and helping to make up, our beliefs about whether there is a supreme intelligence and existence after death or whether love and money keep the world spinning.

The value/power base is the quality, the something, that we refer to when we use few words to describe someone. We say, 'She's a violent person', or 'He is an artistic type', or 'She is a good wife and mother', or 'He is a typical politician', or 'He's a user'.

My real value/power base is the true base for my actions, not the base I want people to think I have or the base that I want to have, or the base that I think I should have.

Stage two adolescents become more aware of there being an ideal value/power base that they can work towards having, a base that they can judge their behaviour against. (This is part of the abstract thinking ability made possible by the change in logical thinking ability mentioned earlier.)

Although kids gradually pick up their own way of doing things, what they like and don't like, and develop their own way of interacting with the world, it is at adolescence that values and power can become a real crisis.

He may know what the parent's values are and be suddenly critical of them, he may be well aware of the values that other people say they have, although they don't behave that way, but he doesn't know what HIS values are. He is just starting to find the values that make him a unique individual.

To do this the young person will experiment with different values to see what he wants to do and doesn't want to do. For a time he may go against values that used to be followed without question, such as going to church.

For the stage one adolescent who continues to hold religious beliefs there will be little difference from childhood beliefs except that God may be seen

"MUM.. MY VALUES SEEM TO BE CHANGING .. I THINK I'LL GIVE SUNDAY-SCHOOL TEACHING THE FLICK.."

as more restrictive than before. The rules of religion may be seen as forbidding all the good things of life.

The stage two adolescent's concept of God changes to a personal God who can be told anything and knows everything about them and still accepts them, even when they do wrong. God becomes the close personal friend. When it seems that parents and friends no longer accept them, the God who knows them better than any parent or friend always accepts them.

Adolescence is a time of change, a time where the values are being blended into a mixture that parents can still greatly influence.

The adult stages of life

There are three other stages of life that I will very mention briefly. They are not important here except that you are no doubt at one of these stages and will be influenced by that in how you react to your children.

The young adult

Young adulthood is seen as being from 21 to 35. Logical thinking is not seen as changing after the change described at stage two adolescence although this change may not occur until after 21.

During the young adult period the personality will gain a level of real love and intimacy as a one to one relationship is formed or there will be a heightened sense of isolation at the failure to form such a relationship. This relationship does not have to be a sexual relationship but could be between the adult and an identity. The young adult may become a priest who has an intimate relationship with God or he may become a businessman who has an intimate relationship with the business world.

A feature of this new stage is the ability to stand back and see himself as separate to the group he belongs to. To objectively examine the group's rules and beliefs and reject them without feeling a loss of self. The young man who got married or became a priest may critically examine the situation and decide to leave, without feeling he has lost his fundamental belief in relationships or Christian outlook.

Adulthood

Adulthood is taken as being from 35 to 60 and is the time of productivity, of generating new life through children or building a business or career.

Through this stage the person will gain a sense of being dynamic and productive or the opposite, of stagnating. There will be a sense of social responsibility , of 'doing her civic duty'. She will join charity groups, help out at the school fete and criticise those who 'don't pull their weight'.

Although committed to group activity, she is also a believer in individual rights, especially when working out right and wrong. She may have started going to church again because she now sees the message of the beliefs as more important than how individuals who claim that belief behave. The religious symbols that lost meaning in the last stage take on a new, deeper meaning.

Maturity

The age of wisdom is seen as being 60 and over. This is a time when a person either looks at what has been done and has a feeling of having acted in accordance with held principles or has a feeling of despair at not having acted that way and at the wasted chances of life.

She now judges things according to universal principles of justice and sees no difference between races and creeds. She can now see that an uneducated person can have a wisdom far greater than that of a highly educated person.

At one end of the scale is the despair of seeing the past as being wasted and having no meaning, of a life spent in pursuit of something that turned out to be false. At the other end of the scale is the person who looks back on life with a feeling of satisfaction, has therefore come to terms with life and because of that has come to terms with death.

Things to think about

✔ Dividing adolescence into two stages, with the first stage being the overlap of childhood and adolescence and the second stage being when 'normal' age-related developments occur, may help parents to a better understanding of their child's behaviour.

✔ Adolescence will see the further development of personality, logical thinking, moral judgement and the value/power base, all of which parents can influence in many ways.

✔ Sexual identity is a major part of the identity crisis teenagers may experience.

✔ In adolescence, the focus of the child's need to belong is likely to shift from the family to the peer group.

✔ This is a crucial time for kids to assess the many values of people around them, at home, school and among their friends, to work out their own value system.

CHAPTER 3

Styles of Discipline

The need for freedom

WHEN CHILDREN REACH the age of 13 to 14, a large number of parents find themselves trying to cope with someone who is staying out all night, smoking dope, drinking alcohol, refusing to keep to mealtimes, being abusive every time they are spoken to, generally disrupting the whole household and giving the younger children the idea that it's OK for teenagers to act that way.

Other parents say the adolescent stage is alright except that the kids are generally lazy, unco-operative, inconsiderate, and contradict everything said to them. Others say everything is OK except for the kids playing their music too loud and not keeping their bedroom tidy. Others say that except for a few isolated incidents there was no stage of rebellion that they noticed in their children at adolescence.

Now, if I were to say that all this is normal and understandable, you would probably think I meant that it is OK. for them to be disruptive and rebellious. No, I am going to say that it is normal and understandable but it is not OK.

They may not understand the vital role that co-operation plays in being independent, because the base that was laid early wasn't developed during childhood and they have not yet developed that concept. 'They have not yet developed that concept' is an important point and is something that should be kept in mind. 'Do they understand?' and, 'Do they know a more responsible way to act?' are questions that need answering.

It is quite normal for the need for freedom to emerge very strongly in early adolescents and for some to act as if it is greater than their sense of belonging to, and dependence on, the family. They generally do not have the sense of responsibility that needs to go with the level of freedom that they demand and this is why there is such disruption to the household.

But don't despair about this rebellion stage because you have already lived through one such stage before with the same child, and survived it. I'm talking about the rebellion that occurred around the age of two or three.

The similarities in behaviour between the two stages are amazing and so are the ways of handling it, because it is the same child. The big difference is that at the earlier stage the child's obvious dependence and need for guidance made the rebellion seem a bit amusing, particularly given that the parent's greater physical power made it so easy to keep control. Now he is too big to stop and the things he is doing are more worrying.

However, you do have the necessary experience to survive again this time and as we go along we will talk more about how to adapt your experience to suit the new situation.

The child's need for freedom seems to be directly opposed to the need for safety, guidance and belonging but the rebellious adolescent still has a strong need to belong and be accepted. This is where the peer group comes in.

As the need for freedom rises, so does the importance of the peer group. The child turns more and more to the peer group to satisfy the need for belonging, for security and identity, or she becomes more and more withdrawn. While the big rebellion is on, the peer group appears to be all-important but most parents find that there is a swing back to the family after a while as the realities of trying to be independent too early start to take effect. Even though the peer group will play a major part from this time on in satisfying the need to belong, there always remains a need to belong to the family.

Parents feel guilty

Generally speaking, when parents are having trouble coping with the behaviour of their children they feel that they have somehow failed. Feelings of guilt and failure can stop parents from seeking help with their problems and these feelings can become worse from remarks made by the many people who seem to think they could have solved the problems so easily.

Extended family members and friends may say, 'Just give him a good thump, that's what he's been asking for'. But many parents have found that using violence, any form of violence, only leaves them feeling even more guilty. Using violence becomes a real temptation, though, when nothing seems to work and the feelings of frustration grow. Other parents just want to leave home.

Parents are very aware that they spend a lot of time trying to correct the behaviour of their children. They try to figure out what went wrong, or more to the point, 'Where did I go wrong?' Probably you didn't go wrong at all. Probably the worst thing you are guilty of is not knowing about something that has influenced the child and because you don't know about it, you cannot be held responsible.

You can't guard a child against every possible word and every possible sight that may have a bad effect but you can be watchful for how he reacts or the ideas he comes out with as a result of contact with other people, TV and the media.

The media puts great pressure on young people to perform well in many things, from sex to sport. The commercial world just tries to make money out of them in any way it can and doesn't seem to care about the effect on the kids. Advertisements constantly tell them they are worthless unless they have the latest fad or use some product or other.

The adult world may be putting tremendous pressure on the kids to star at sport and school, and to avoid sex and drugs. However, there are not enough jobs at the end of school and the message that teenagers can get from the adult world is to go for casual sex and drugs but don't get caught.

Some parents feel that they are the only ones who have troubles with their children and are ashamed to seek help. They feel that there is some shame to admitting that they are having trouble handling or understanding some behaviours. The fact is that no-one in the world understands all the behaviour of kids or adults.

Some children who misbehave or are difficult to handle turn out to have been sexually abused at some time and have felt unable, too ashamed, too guilty or too frightened to tell anyone. If this is discovered with some kids, how many others who are misbehaving do so as a result of being abused?

Some kids really believe they have told their parents about being sexually abused and were not believed even though in fact they have never mentioned it. This can come about as a result of the child's self-centred outlook causing her to believe the conversations she holds in her head have actually occurred or are known by the parent.

One girl used to be 'felt up' by her uncle as she sat on his knee at the kitchen table. The combination of the mother's encouragement to sit on the uncle's knee and the girl's belief that what she was aware of was also known to others

in the room meant that, to her, the mother approved of what the uncle was doing to her under the table. Without being told about the uncle's actions, a parent could wonder forever what she did wrong to cause her child to be so resentful of her, when in fact it was not her fault.

Another girl believed she had revealed being abused by a neighbour but in fact she had only told her mother about the neighbour giving her lollies.

On a lighter note, there was the boy who would not go to sleep without the light on and would wake up the moment the light was switched off. Years later he told me that the reason was that some adult had said to him that when you go to bed the Sandman comes along and throws sand in your eyes to make you sleepy. No way was he having anyone sneak up on him in the dark and throw sand in his eyes.

There was the man who would never sing at church or in any group and this he said was the result of one belittling remark made by a teacher about his singing at school.

Two things can be learnt from this. Firstly, how careful all adults should be about what they say to children and secondly, that there are so many possible causes of a child's behaviour that it is ridiculous for parents to automatically blame themselves.

A few points about stages of life

Just before considering the three different types of discipline to use with kids I want to make a few points about stages in general.

Friends say, 'Don't worry, it's just a stage she's going through' and they could be dead right. However, according to the idea of stages, once she has moved to the new stage of thinking and feeling, there is no way back.

This is no different to physical changes because once a person has grown from a baby to a school kid there is no way to go back to being a baby. Once a person has gained a new way of thinking and feeling there is no return to the old ways, unless he suffers brain damage. Another similarity between the physical and the psychological/emotional development is that a person goes through the baby size, then the childhood size, then the teenage size, as he moves towards the adult size. Each physical stage has to be gone through in turn and a stage cannot be skipped.

Psychological/emotional development is the same, each stage has to be gone through in turn and a stage can't be skipped. The problem is that we can't see what stage a person is at in the psychological/emotional development and sometimes we expect more than the person is capable of, or we might underestimate what they are capable of understanding.

What we are calling the first stage of adolescence would normally be expected before the age of 13 and usually the second stage sneaks in at about 15. However, many children of 13 or 14 will display the characteristics described in the second stage and many children of 17 or 18 (or 50) will display the characteristics described in the first stage. The ages are used more as a convenience of explanation rather than for how a person should think or act at a particular age. The only thing that is certain is that stage one and two must come in that order, even though a person may spend a very short time or a very long time at stage one.

The main point to be made here is that a person in stage one adolescence is not capable of thinking, seeing, or judging like a person in the second stage of adolescence but the second stager is capable of thinking, seeing and judging like an early adolescent. Confusing? Not really. Think about it as comparing an adult to a little child, the child can't think, see, or make judgements like the adult can but the adult can sure think, see and judge like a little child sometimes.

You can't put an old head on young shoulders and you can't put a stage two adolescent's head on a stage one adolescent's shoulders. This means there are differences in what should be expected from each person and differences in how certain behaviours can be treated.

As mentioned above there may be only a very short time spent in stage one, or a young person may get 'stuck' there, but it is possible to assist development to the second stage of adolescence and further by stimulating the child's thinking, getting her to solve moral problems (making up rules) and looking at things in different ways. Generally, this will mean always talking to the young person as if he is already at stage two adolescence. It is important to take this position because it's too difficult to decide if he is at stage one or stage two. In doing this you are working to help him develop and the above explanation is to help you see that the child does need your parenting during the adolescent stage of life. He may not want it but he definitely needs it.

Gardeners know that the time to train plants and shrubs is during a time of change. Once the tree is grown it is extremely difficult to change its shape but it is relatively easy while the tree is growing. Adolescence is a wonderful chance for parents to correct influences from the past and greatly influence the eventual outcome of their parenting, and it is a pity that so many miss the opportunity by arguing and fighting with the kids. Arguing and fighting are the very things that will have the opposite effect to what is really needed at this stage.

When parents and children argue they are usually very busy thinking up reasons to justify doing the things they are doing or thinking the way they think, or acting the way they are already acting. Therefore, efforts to 'win' an argument may be at the expense of delaying the development of the child. It is far better to present sometimes conflicting alternatives, thoughts and ideas and allow or encourage kids to make decisions about those alternatives. Adolescence is a time of intelligent and sensitive experimentation, so keep feeding them the sort of information you want them to base these experiments on.

Three stages of discipline

If we lived in an ideal world parents would know the three discipline styles and at what ages to use each of them. Once a child had reached the appropriate age in the ideal world, the new discipline style would be started and the old style dropped.

Unfortunately we do not live in an ideal world and we know from the description of stages that a person aged 16 (or 60) can throw a 2-year-old type tantrum to get what he wants but a child of two is not capable of operating at the same level as that of the 16-year-old.

Another problem in our imperfect world is that the 16-year-old may not have developed in moral thinking past the 10-year-old stage and yet be advanced in other ways.

However, for simplicity, I will put the idea of the three styles of discipline as if we do live in a perfect world.

The first style is called *intervention*. This simply means that the parent is stepping in to provide for the needs of the child, and to guide, teach, direct and correct the behaviour of the child so that his behaviour is within what is considered socially acceptable behaviour. In short, it means the parent is making the rules.

The second style is called *interaction*. This means that the parent and the child are working and talking together to solve the problems associated with meeting the child's needs and to work out how and when things should be done. In short, it means the parent and the child are deciding on the rules.

The third style is called *non-intervention*. This means it is time for the parent to sit back and observe how the child is solving his problems but be there with assistance, opinions and suggested alternative strategies when appropriate. In short, the child is making the rules.

Generally speaking, the intervention style is best with preschoolers, kids up to the age of six. The interaction style is best with primary school kids, aged from 6 to 12 years old. The non-intervention style is best with secondary school kids, aged from 13 upwards.

Remember, we are talking about an ideal world, something that does not exist. In the real world you may have the problem of a 13-year-old wanting the freedom of an adult and disrupting the whole household as he threatens his younger brothers and sisters to get his own way. Obviously you could not sit back and just observe as you wait for him to approach you for an opinion. However, at the moment I will ask you to bear with me as I continue with my ideal world.

INTERVENTION

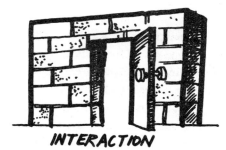

INTERACTION

NON-INTERVENTION

Intervention

The preschooler does not have what we call logical thinking ability, he lives in a world of imagination and magic. He believes in Santa Claus and the Easter Bunny. He has to be taught everything from feeding himself to tying his own shoelaces and dressing himself.

He needs to be shown how to do everything, even though he learns a great deal from copying what he sees others doing. The time from 18 months to 6 years old is when the main socialising is done as the child learns to share, to ask 'properly', to eat with a knife and fork, to say 'please' and 'thank you'.

It is a time when he is stopped from touching heaters and power points, guided to discover what the word 'hot' means, not allowed to ride his bike without a helmet, has toys taken from him if he misbehaves, gets taken to the doctor, is given immunisation injections, is bribed with ice-creams and lollies, goes where the family want to go and when they want to go, is taken to the playground and told which things he can play on.

Showing, directing, guiding, ordering, steering, punishing, rewarding, teaching and stopping are all intervention words and are quite rightly used a great deal in parenting preschoolers. The parents have to make the rules when the kids are small because the kids don't realise the dangers or understand the problems that the rules solve. It would take forever to arrive at solutions to problems trying to work them out with preschoolers. Parents try for a while but eventually come to, 'That's how it is and no arguments'. The child's normal reaction is, 'But why?' Parents also try to answer this one but after the fifteenth 'why' they resort to, 'Because I said so, that's why, now just do it'.

This is perfectly all right at this stage, it is the stage of intervention, of directing the behaviour of the child. Some parents can be afraid of being accused of child abuse if they direct their children or restrict them in any way but their very fear of this may be causing them to abuse their children in the opposite way. One of the ways to abuse children is by neglect and one of the ways to neglect children is to fail to give them sufficient discipline.

Discipline means to keep within certain limits of behaviour and if a child is not mature enough to keep himself within those limits then it is the duty of the adults responsible for that child to teach him what the limits are and to use ways of keeping him within those limits. The parent has to help him become aware of the benefits of keeping within those limits and the consequences of going outside those limits. Getting a child to keep within certain limits of behaviour is part of expressing love and caring for a child. The method used in getting him to keep within those limits, however, may be child abuse.

Discipline is necessary for a child to feel secure and loved, to belong. Discipline is good, self-discipline is better but self-discipline in all things is beyond a preschooler. He is getting there and has more self-discipline at five than he had at two but he still needs a lot of direction to keep within the lines.

Time out and quiet time

When it is necessary to impose some penalty, the most effective method at this stage is 'time out' or 'quiet time'. In fact, variations of these are effective at any age and we will talk about that in later chapters too.

Quiet time simply means getting the child to go to a particular position and remain there for a set time or until a certain condition has been met; for

instance, telling a child to sit on a chair a little apart from whatever the activity is, 'Until you calm down'. Another way is to do the same but say, 'Until you have been quiet for two minutes'. Another way is to say, 'Until you have controlled yourself for five minutes'. When using this method you must be sure to have the child remain in the quiet time position until the conditions have been met.

Time out is different in that the child is sent to a place more removed from the action and this may be another room. The things said about the length of time and any conditions in imposing the quiet time can also be said in regard to time out. Try to make sure that the place the child is sent to for time out hasn't got too many interesting things in the area otherwise it may be a fun place to be. The bedroom isn't normally a good place because usually there are toys in a bedroom.

As he gets closer to six there is less need to be directing him and explanations for the rules or directions are accepted without question, even if the explanation is not fully understood. This is because he is beginning to accept the necessity for rules. (Remember I am still in an ideal world.)

Interaction

Seven is the age of reason, when a child has developed the capacity to see the order of things and can see that one thing causes another. From the previous chapter we know that he has advanced in being able to see things from someone else's point of view but is still very self-centred. The stage is set for him to take more responsibility for his own life through having more say in what he does and how he does it.

The time has come for the parent and the child to share the decision making by working out together the what and how and when and where. The ideal is for all the household to join in discussions at a 'family meeting' and decisions made at that meeting would apply until changed at another meeting.

In fact, the family meeting method works extremely well for many families. Some do it on a formal level and have a set time and place for the meeting, other families use the method but have meetings as a problem arises. Others discuss problems at mealtimes in what appears to be an informal way but is really a deliberate strategy introduced by the parents.

The difficult part for parents in this 'interaction' business is that often the solution seems obvious and it is much quicker to just make the rules and get on with the hundred and one other things to be done.

When the child used to throw tantrums you made an investment for the future when you put up with the noise and embarrassment and feelings of guilt as you ignored his antics because the result was worth the effort. Life became more pleasant for you when the tantrums stopped and they stopped when they no longer worked for the child. Life also became more pleasant for the child.

The time spent on interaction between you and the kids is a similar investment for the future, it can save a great deal of time and trouble. It can result in a much more settled household where you can get on with life instead of spending most of the time trying to control the kids. Some parents spend hours each day just sorting out the problems and misbehaviour of the kids, when a little time spent each week on interaction about problems could save most of that time for other interests and activities.

As we go into this more in later chapters I hope to show that it is well worth putting off other things to spend a little time on interaction.

The age between 7 and 12 is the time when the child is most interested in order and what causes what and this means he is interested in the rules about life. He wants to know how to use tools, and rules are the tools for solving problems. Show him how to use the tool called rules, give him practice at it now and he will have that skill for life. It's like learning to ride a bike or swimming, once he has the skill, he has it for life.

Although the keen interest in rules makes this the best age for interaction to work, there will still be times when some form of discipline has to be imposed if a child is not behaving well and not being co-operative. In general, the same methods used in the previous stage will work here because the child's belief in authority figures means he is inclined to follow directions, probably more so than in the previous stage.

However, as we will see later, co-operation, sharing and the natural consequences of behaviour are an important part of the interaction period.

Quiet time and time out are still the most severe 'punishments' that a parent can impose and the child will generally keep to the conditions of the quiet time and time out as long as it doesn't stretch into a long time. Unless you are waiting out a tantrum, very short times are sufficient – just long enough for him to get control of himself. A point can be made in a few minutes of time out but the same point can be wrecked in an hour's time out. The aim isn't to break the kid, the aim is for him to get control of himself.

Non-intervention

Ah! Heaven at last. The time when the child turns 13 and the parent can sit back and watch him solve his problems, with only an occasional need to give an opinion or make a suggestion, and then only because the child has asked for the opinion.

He has a firm grasp of rules and why they are there. He has become practiced at solving problems and needs little or no need for intervention. Interaction is easy because he can now see things from other people's point of view and can allow for their needs. He also has a deep need to belong and wants to please people.

The young person is now able to work out many different ways to solve the one problem and gets most of his guidance from the peer group. In general, discipline is the result of experiencing the consequences of his own behaviour and the parent is the silent observer of this process.

On the rare occasions when some outside discipline is required, and interaction has not worked, variations of what worked at the 2-year-old stage will work now. Quiet time and time out remain the most dreaded consequences at any age and as long as the method is used in an appropriate way it gets results without damaging the relationship.

Non-intervention can be the hardest discipline method for a parent to use because parents find it difficult to accept it as being discipline. Many parents see non-intervention as allowing the child to 'get away with it'. Other parents find it too difficult to let the child 'take the consequences' and see it as their duty to save him.

Where to now?

It isn't an ideal world and the fact is that all three styles of discipline have to be used at all stages of a child's development. There are times when a parent has to step back and allow a 2-year-old to 'take the consequences' and there are times when a teenager has to be firmly guided in behaviour. So why group the disciplines into the ages as I have?

There should be more intervention-type parenting for the preschoolers than interaction and non-intervention. There should be more interaction-type parenting for the primary school child than intervention or non-intervention. There should be more non-intervention-type parenting for the teenager than intervention or interaction.

For all stages there is a need for guidance and teaching and loving and encouragement and discipline. There is never a need for shaming or ridicule or lack of respect or taking away the dignity of a child.

The rest of this book will try to help parents to choose what discipline style they want to use and when. In other words, the aim is for parents to feel they have control over their parenting so they can help their children's social and moral development.

Things to think about

✔ It is quite normal for the need for freedom to emerge strongly in early adolescence and for some teenagers to act as if this is greater than their sense of belonging to and dependence on the family.

✔ There are too many things that can happen in the life of a child to influence his behaviour for parents to be able to guard against them all, but they can take care in what they say to him, watch his reactions and help him change his inappropriate behaviour.

✔ Some children who are difficult to handle have been sexually abused at some time and feel too ashamed or guilty to tell anyone.

✔ Using the appropriate styles of discipline from the early stages in a child's development can help the child develop appropriate styles of behaviour in adolescence.

CHAPTER 4

Moral Development

Should parents pass on moral values?

S O FAR WE HAVE been following four lines in child development. This chapter will single out moral development, probably because it is the hardest and most controversial subject to tackle. I want to state that not only is it possible for parents to help the moral development of their children, but it is also essential to do so. Parents need to know what their own moral values are as the need for parents to give their children moral guidance becomes more important in a world that seems to have 'lost the plot' when it comes to morals.

Many parents have come to believe that they have no right to try to pass on values to their children because many of those values are classed as 'a matter of morals'. Of course it's a matter of morals but what better could a parent do than help a child develop a high level of moral thinking? The problem is that the parents need a base for their own moral judgements, a base that is acceptable in a society fast losing the old religious base.

Parents who allow themselves to be pressured by other people can find themselves being told they must alter their moral standards to allow for the changing morals of modern times, that the old moral attitudes are now old-fashioned and parents should not be imposing those outmoded standards onto their kids. Their idea is that children should be allowed to make up their own minds about moral standards.

Many parents are perplexed at being urged to go against their beliefs and better judgement to allow their teenagers to do things such as bring casual sex partners home for the night. Parents are supposed to have a broader outlook on life and to realise that, because their children are going to have sex anyway, the parents should make sure the kids are well educated in sexual matters and make it easy for them to have sex under safe conditions. The argument is that it is not really encouraging them to have sex because they were going to anyway, it is only being realistic about it. By this sort of reasoning, we should therefore change any of our standards if it can be shown that people will do it anyway.

It is increasingly difficult to know what is right and wrong in this world of ours as everything changes so rapidly and there are so many opinions on the subject. We live in a society that is made up of people from every country in the world who find it difficult knowing right from wrong because of cultural and religious differences between each other. Certain cultural practices can also differ from the law of the land.

The answer to very complicated situations often turns out to be very simple and I believe this is true of this most complicated of subjects, maybe not on a national or international level but certainly at the family and interpersonal level.

First of all I want to look at the meaning of the word 'moral' so that we know what we're talking about. The word 'moral' seems to be too often thought of as something to do with sex, so that referring to someone as having low morals would mean being sexually active and not caring much who with.

The word 'moral' really means making a distinction between right and wrong; sex is only one of the things that we have to make a decision on as to what's right and what's wrong.

Any decision at all about right and wrong is a moral decision and this applies to any behaviour in our daily lives, including all of the behaviour of people towards each other. Lying and stealing, cheating, love, charity, talking, and any other behaviour. Every word and every action of every person in their day-to-day living is subject to moral judgement because every action has an effect on someone or something.

Moral development at preschool age

Where does moral development start? We saw in Chapter 1 that the beginnings of moral thinking occur as the child becomes aware of being separate to the rest of the world and he then has to work out what the relationship is between himself and the rest of the world. Again, I'm not trying to insult your intelligence by claiming a child thinks, 'Oh, I am becoming separate from . . .' I mean that about the same time as he becomes aware that there are rules about

" WHILE YOU WERE AT CAMP WE RE-DECORATED YOUR ROOM. "

putting words together, the child develops a sense that there are rules of behaviour and he develops a sense of either, 'Rules are good things that give me security and let me know I belong' or, 'Rules are bad things that restrict me and hurt me because I am bad'.

At that stage rules are kept to because the big people said so and the big people get mad and punish him when he doesn't obey the rules. On the other hand, the big people are happy and give him good things when he obeys the rules.

This is not true moral thinking because it is only centred on himself, there is no real ability to consider the other person because he hasn't yet developed the ability to see things from another person's point of view. However, getting a strong awareness of the existence of rules is the basis for moral development.

Primary school age moral development

This awareness of rules and the ability to reason is what makes *interaction* possible for the 6-to-12-year-old and beyond. There is more ability to see things from another person's point of view and this has to be encouraged and strengthened for her moral development.

The whole idea of interaction is to increase the child's awareness of the effect his behaviour has on himself and other people and the effect other people's behaviour has on him. Moral development comes from solving moral dilemmas, the everyday dilemma of balancing his needs against the needs of others.

'Dilemma' is just another word for 'problem' and it is the practice at solving problems of what is right and wrong that strengthens moral thinking. The more practice a person gets at doing something the better they can do it.

Between 6 to 12 years old, kids become very aware of the usefulness of rules, of putting things in order, that rules are solutions to problems. Preschool kids see wrong behaviour as being behaviour that is punished and right behaviour as being behaviour that is rewarded but primary school kids see right behaviour as behaviour that keeps within the rules and wrong behaviour as behaviour that breaks the rules.

This is a major change in moral thinking because now he can see that even though his behaviour was right, because he kept to the rule, he might still get punished. For example, the teacher punishes the whole class because the culprit didn't own up.

The preschooler judges how wrong a behaviour is from the reaction of adults. The primary school kid comes to realise that there can be rules made about punishments as well as about behaviour and the reaction of adults is not a good guide as to the seriousness of a behaviour. Rules can be made to 'make the time fit the crime'. Some adults keep referring to punishments as 'consequences' but at this age it means the same thing.

As the ability to use logical thinking develops so does the ability to argue about whether he did break the rule or not and he can go into great detail. Sometimes the logic may not make much sense to you but this is when it's important to try to see things from the child's point of view, simply because that's how he sees it. Seeing things from his point of view does not mean that you agree, it simply means you are clear about what it is you disagree with and can insist on your point of view being heard.

To further the moral development of the primary school child, the combination of their ability to see things from another person's point of view and seeing rules as important. needs to be encouraged. Giving kids practice at making rules to solve problems of how to behave in regard to other people and the environment is strengthening their moral development.

Primary school justice is generally on an 'eye for an eye' basis and this seems to work in favour of the school bullies who are protected by the great universal rule of 'never put ánybody in'. The rule conscious primary school age is the base for the real caring, sharing and co-operation that is necessary for a strong social conscience to develop and is also the base for the development of real criminal antisocial behaviour.

The assertive use of interaction to give children practice at making rules teaches caring, sharing and co-operation but allowing the natural self-centredness of the child to dominate the making of the rules will result in that self-centredness growing.

Although primary school children can see things from the other person's point of view, it doesn't mean they can understand the other person's feelings very much or that they can understand the underlying meanings in what happens. To help them develop to the next stage in moral development, these things need to be pointed out and explained to them.

Parents who become discouraged about their kids not understanding about people's feelings and about hidden meanings may stop explaining about them and so miss out on the opportunities to help their moral development. Kids who find it difficult to understand about feelings and meanings are being normal but they need to hear about these things because development occurs from trying to understand. The fact that he doesn't understand is a good reason to stimulate his thinking by throwing in some 'one liners' about feelings and meanings.

Adolescent moral development

The time that I call Stage One adolescence is the time when the child is struggling to understand this business of feelings, meaning and motives in behaviour, to understand what is happening to the body, to cope with changing from primary to secondary school and the difference in the work, to cope with the change in sexual and social pressures heaped on kids and trying to come to terms with all the new feelings.

This is the turmoil time, when the new adolescent is using the old ways of thinking in trying to understand so many new things, and so much is just not fitting in. If the child is able to make sense of it all using the present way of thinking he may not develop to the 'scientific' stage of logical thinking and therefore cannot develop to the next stage of moral development. If the turmoil time is resolved using the old logic he may go right through life and cope very well without developing further. It doesn't mean he is a lesser person, it just means he works things out in a different way.

For some stage one adolescents consideration of other people takes a nosedive and he can go right off the rails for a time. This can be seen in different ways; one is that the child is rebelling against having to balance his needs against other people's needs; another is that he is experiencing the crisis of feeling alone and insecure, a feeling that often results in young people lashing out.

Lying can become a real problem at this stage. With some kids any resemblance to the truth in anything they say is purely by chance and lying becomes just a way of manipulating to get his own way. With others, truth and 'being trusted' becomes the important thing.

If his thinking does change to the abstract thinking of what I have called Stage Two adolescence and he has had enough practice using rules in making decisions he will probably develop in moral thinking to the stage where a person's motive becomes important and people become more important than rules.

A child entering adolescence finds the task of making and holding friends much easier if he has gained a strong regard for rules earlier. This is because the moral thinking of the stage two adolescent is about the rules of the role he is playing and most of the roles are social roles. The peer group, family, even school becomes a place for socialising and that is why considering other people's needs makes life easier for him.

Because he is so occupied with finding his own identity he is also becoming more aware of how different he is to other people. Developing a greater ability to see things from another person's point of view means being capable of feeling real emotional empathy with people. Empathy is the ability to put yourself in the other person's position, to feel what they feel and see things as they see them.

Rules are still very important, especially those that guide interpersonal relationships and those that make the various roles clear. The stage two adolescent is likely to judge his own and other people's behaviour according to how he sees a person in that position should act. He is conscious of how a good scout or good son or good catholic should act and can be quite harsh in that judgement.

Contrary to what people generally think about adolescence, the change in moral thinking at later adolescence is to being conventional, being the same as others, becoming part of their society. Teenagers claim to rebel against convention but in fact the basis of their moral thinking develops into the opposite to what they claim. It is a time of conforming to the rules of the peer group and to the music and fashion fads of the day. That's why they all dress and talk alike. It is a time of becoming 'like everybody else'.

This conformity to the peer group is a very important and necessary part of moral development and should be encouraged because it is helping them become part of the society, to belong.

We already know that adolescents need outside control even if they don't want it from their parents. They usually transfer that need onto the peer group and take more notice of their friends than of their parents. This is one of the necessary steps in the process of breaking away from the parents. It is the process of passing their need for outside guidance and control over to society in general, to the law and the rules of the groups to which they belong and then, as they get older, the need for control will hopefully be converted to self-control.

" *I KNOW NICOLE IS JUST CONFORMING TO PEER GROUP PRESSURE, BUT I DO WISH SHE WAS.. WELL.. ..A LITTLE MORE 'CONFORMIST.'* "

What moral guidelines can we teach kids?

By now I hope I have convinced you of the need for kids to be involved in deciding what the rules are going to be for the house, or the school, or the games they play. What remains now is to talk about what can guide parents in helping kids develop a sense of responsibility to other people when they are making rules, and maybe even to help them feel a little guilty when they do something wrong.

We have to tackle this problem of morals because we are going to be looking at some tough subjects like setting limits and negotiating rules for teenage behaviour as well as appropriate consequences for when those limits are broken.

Anybody who speaks out about right and wrong is immediately branded as 'moralising' and I suppose that's correct because it is talking about what people should do and what they shouldn't do, but it's also true that people need a guide as to how to behave when there are no rules about a particular activity, or when there are conflicting possibilities.

No matter what age we are, we still have a need for rules and guidelines of behaviour. If we don't have those rules or don't know the rules we feel unsafe and don't know how to act.

The great difficulty for me in talking to you about moral behaviour is that I don't know what your religious beliefs are or what your culture is and I don't know where you live. Your religious and cultural background makes a big difference to what you think is right and wrong. So does the locality you live in because what is legal in one State is illegal in another.

Many people use the law as their guide for making moral decisions but they have to change their moral thinking as the law changes or if they move to an area that has different laws. Therefore, the law is not a good base for me to put forward as the guide in making moral decisions.

To me, the main religions hold the answer but it isn't practical for any one religion to be put forward as the moral base because we would spend the next few hundred years arguing as to which religion should be used as the base and then, just as we came to an agreement, the atheists would put their bid in to do away with all religion anyway, and we would be back where we started. There is enough religious strife in the world without us adding to it here, so I think we had better consider another way.

Some people would say we could use our conscience as the base, that we just 'know' what is right or wrong because there is a little voice inside us that whispers the answer. This appears to work quite well but sometimes I wonder if we only hear what we want to hear from that little voice, and I wonder if the only reason we decide it's wrong is because the little voice says, 'You'll get caught!'. There also seems to be another little voice that urges us to disregard the first little voice and I have trouble knowing which little voice to trust. To me, there has to be a better way than 'hearing voices' to decide if an action is right or wrong.

What makes a behaviour 'wrong'?

Before we get to the base for judging right from wrong we need to spend a little time deciding just what it is that makes a behaviour 'wrong'.

The most common answer given to a question like, 'Why is it wrong for a 15-year-old to be drinking in a pub?' is that it is against the law. This is a good example of how we have become brainwashed to look at right and wrong behaviour as being within or outside the law. The main wrong done is the actual breaking of the law, whereas when the law was first made it must have been made for a reason.

Maybe the reason many adults don't think about why some rules were made is because for many generations society and the church have stressed the importance of keeping to the rules and people didn't get much encouragement to make rules. The authority figures at school, at church and at home made the rules and we had to stick to them, 'or else!'

Those days are gone and the kids ask damn stupid questions like, 'But why is it wrong?' Panic!! We try the old , 'Because I said so, that's why' which used to work for our parents but now only brings a contemptuous look from the kids. Another reason we don't know why a law was made is because the particular way of doing something has become a tradition that is just the way it's done. 'It's always been that way, that's why', 'Because it's wrong to break the law'.

None of these replies actually explains why the behaviour is wrong. The message behind them is, 'You have broken the law and you have to be punished'. This may account for why so many people believe that the only thing they did wrong was to get caught. They may have broken the rule many times and the only time it was a bother was when they were caught. Therefore, the logical thing to do is to get better at not getting caught.

The behaviour of some adults is very little different to the behaviour of kids when it comes to law-breaking and paying the consequences. A woman once told me that her brother was serving a jail sentence, 'Because his mate was a dog [an informer]'. When I suggested that what she said meant that the magistrate had pronounced, 'I sentence you to jail because your friend is a dog', she looked at me as if I was stupid. When I suggested that the magistrate had sent him to jail because of his behaviour in robbing someone, she then argued about the number of people who steal and don't go to jail because they don't get caught.

In her logic her brother was in jail only because he got caught and he wouldn't have been caught if his friend hadn't been an informer. We had quite a long discussion about our different ways of looking at it but I don't know if her opinion changed, and she certainly didn't change my opinion that the real reason her brother was in jail was because of his stealing behaviour.

The idea that 'breaking the rules' is what is wrong about a behaviour is the moral thinking of the stage one adolescent but stage two says that people are more important than rules, so we have to use a base for making moral decisions that takes that level of thinking into account.

For something to be truly 'wrong' it would have to be universally wrong and not just a socially unacceptable thing that can change from day to day. Anything that is wrong has to be wrong for anyone to do anywhere, and if the behaviour is not universally wrong for any human to do then it is more a question of it being socially unacceptable rather than wrong. When something is socially unacceptable, it can be changed one way or the other at any time by the powers that be at the time, but when something is wrong, it's wrong no matter who is in power and no matter where in the world it is done.

The rules of a household usually cover behaviours that are acceptable or unacceptable for that household and can be changed one way or the other by the people in that household.

A base for making moral decisions

Fortunately there are two things that are universally wrong, easily identified and simple enough to use for you to have complete confidence in any argument with any person who questions your choice of limits and rules.

Simple enough for you to be able to use when you're under pressure to explain why a particular rule has been made, or to be a guide for you when you have to think up a rule in a hurry.

1 It is wrong to deny people a fair go (physically, emotionally, psychologically, spiritually).

2 It is wrong to place people in any sort of danger (physically, emotionally, psychologically, spiritually).

Things that are wrong can only be things that are considered to be wrong in the fundamental tenets of all cultures and in all religions and, to my present knowledge, this applies to anything that threatens the right of people to feel safe and the right of people to a fair go at what is available for the satisfaction of their basic needs and wants.

In other words the physical, emotional, psychological, and spiritual safety of people must be protected from violation and the rights of people to a social, educational, recreational, and economic fair go must be protected from violation by other people.

The concept of 'a fair go' may need a little explanation. The concept would be best described as 'having the right to an equal opportunity to get an equal share' of something. Whether the person wanted to put effort into getting that equal share would then be up to him. It very definitely does NOT mean 'having the right to an equal share' of something.

Safety and A Fair Go together cover all of a parent or child's needs, wants, interests, responsibilities, duties, fears and anxieties. There will be a mixture of these things whenever a parent and child are trying to work out a rule. Therefore we can make life easier for ourselves by making an easy to remember rule about making rules.

'All rules must be explainable using the concepts of A Fair Go and Safety'.

By using the idea of a fair go and safety when asked a question like, 'But why that rule?', all that needs to be considered is whether the rule is made as

"AS YOUR MOTHER, DON'T I DESERVE A FAIR GO?"
"AW— FAIR GO, MUM!"

a matter of safety or to give people a fair go, or maybe a bit of both. Simply ask yourself, 'What would this rule come under, A Fair Go or Safety?'

The answer would include how the breaking of this rule would affect other people, whether that effect was direct, through other people, or through an effect on the environment. In a household, the household is the environment and therefore any effect on the general running of the house affects everyone in it.

A Fair Go and Safety means the rights of a person to a fair go and safety in regard to every part of their personal and social life. Every person in the house has interests and pressures from within themselves, from others in the house and from outside the house and these interests and pressures all have to be considered in making the rules of the house. This is still a tall order, even when we have a simple tool like A Fair Go and Safety to help work it out.

To do harm to a person in any way is wrong and, although I believe in strict discipline, I believe the punishment (revenge) system uses one or other of physical, emotional, psychological, and spiritual harm in the attempt to change a person's behaviour. Parents who use rewards and punishments to control their children can easily drop into the habit of using a slap, belittlement, ridicule, or maybe attack a child's way of relating to the world, and all of these things are abuse.

Getting a rule changed

If you cannot think of a way that the rule fits in with the idea of safety or a fair go then the rule should be changed, or dropped, because it serves no useful purpose and is probably just a value difference. However, even the changing of a rule is covered by the rule of A Fair Go and Safety.

Just saying that a rule or limit is stupid or useless doesn't mean that it should be disobeyed, the rule about making rules means that the old rule applies until a new one is made and the changing of rules must be done in a way that protects people's safety and gives them a fair go.

If there isn't a set procedure for getting a law changed no-one would be safe. Many people would feel justified in disregarding any law seen as silly, or if they couldn't see how it protected people, or if this gave them a better deal. Given that people are self-centred in their motives, it isn't hard to imagine that many would deliberately ignore the reasons for laws simply so they could disobey them for their own gain, usually at the expense of someone else.

If there is no agreed way for a child to get a rule changed or for the child to have a say, he will have to draw attention to his problem somehow, and this is usually by misbehaving in some way.

I strongly believe that a group or society is only as strong as the dedication of it's members to the rules of the group or society and therefore the breaking of the rules should be treated as a serious thing. However, when it comes to families, the breaking of rules should be dealt with because of the effect that the breaking of rules has on the family members. In other words, the breaking of the rules should not be the central focus, the central focus should be on the reason the rule was made in the first place.

This is entirely different to saying that something is wrong because it's against the rules, but it seems to be a very difficult adjustment to make in our thinking.

Examples of rules using the Fair Go and Safety base

Let's have a look at some normal house rules and see how the Fair Go and Safety rule works.

RULE
'The evening meal is at six o'clock and everyone is to be home by then'.

A Fair Go or Safety? Clearly the easiest way to explain the reason for this rule comes under Fair Go, so that:

■ There isn't a waste of food.
■ The effort of the person cooking isn't belittled.
■ Power isn't wasted by people cooking at all different times.
■ The cost of cooking is minimised so there is money available for other things.

There is an element of Safety in this rule as well because:

■ The person cooking can monitor the balanced diet being received by members of the family.
■ If there is a set meeting time for members of the family there is a known opportunity for problems to be discussed.
■ There is also the opportunity for the parents to count heads and know that everyone is safe and well.
■ Routine can give every member of the family the confidence of knowing what is happening at any given time.

Clearly a very good argument can be put forward for a set mealtime that doesn't need the 'Because I said so' answer. Other rules that are to do with time limits could be explained in much the same way.

RULE
'There is to be no smoking in the house'.

There are many reasons for such a rule and they come under both Fair Go and Safety. Smell, hindrance to breathing, health, danger, burn damage, messiness.

RULE
'Mother will only wash clothes placed
in the laundry'.

This one would come under a Fair Go for Mother (with a possibility of Safety under the health heading so she doesn't have to go into the smelly bedroom).

RULE
'Night curfew is 1 a.m.'.

Disputes over curfews are probably the most common conflicts between parents and adolescent children.

The following come to mind from the reasons given by one particular mother for insisting on a curfew for her 15-year-old-daughter:

■ To know that daughter is safe. (Safety.)

■ Mother's parental responsibility is to set guidelines of acceptable behaviour. (Fair Go for Mother's duty of care.)

■ When she comes in late she wakes up the younger kids. (Fair Go for other kids in house.)

■ Mother needs to make sure the house is secure before she can sleep. (Safety of household, Fair Go because it's unfair to keep Mother awake late, duty of care.)

■ Daughter having own key is no good because she loses it and the finder then has access to the house. (Safety.)

RULE
'Always wash your hands before
touching food'.

Any rule to do with health comes very much under the Safety banner, whether it is for the health of the young person or other people, and doing things that could result in spreading infection also comes under Fair Go.

The above are just a few rules to give you some idea of how the Fair Go and Safety idea works but there is no way we can cover all of the possibilities.

Very emotional subjects such as abortion, sex, and forms of contraception are to do with health so discussions and arguments should all be based on A Fair Go and Safety issues. The same applies to the use of alcohol, tobacco and other drugs.

In general, how can you work out what the problem comes under, A Fair Go or Safety?

It can be a little hard to work this out at first until you become used to it so I have made two lists below, one is of words that tend to be used when there is a high Fair Go aspect to the problem and the other is of words that tend to be used when there is a high Safety aspect to the problem. The separation is not as clear-cut as it appears from the lists because many of the words could be used in either section. However, they tend to be used more in regard to one than the other.

Words that are used when there is a Fair Go problem.

Accuse	Discussion	Late	Responsible
Agree	Disobey	Listen	Right
Agreement	Donate	Love	Rights
Aid	Early	Mine	Rule
Allow	Encourage	Moral	Share
Assertive	Enough	Negotiate	Steal
Assist	Equal	No	Steer
Bias	Fail	Obey	Stubborn
Blame	Gift	Onus	Submit
Caring	Give	Order	Subordinate
Cheat	Guide	Ours	Take
Communicate	Help	Own	Tenderness
Consider	Hers	Possess	Theirs
Co-operate	His	Prejudice	Too little
Dictate	Inconsiderate	Property	Too much
Direct	Irresponsible	Punctual	Unequal
Disagree	Just	Reconcile	Wrong
Discriminate	Keep	Refuse	Yours

Words that tend to be used when there is a Safety problem.

Abuse	Cut	Hit	Risk
Accident	Danger	Hurt	Roads
Accuse	Dark	Hygiene	Safety
Alcohol	Disease	Infect	Sex
Ambulance	Diving	Insult	Sick
Assault	Drugs	Kill	Smack
Assist	Epidemic	Knife	Smoke
Baton	Fall	Moral	Sneer
Belittle	Fear	Mull	Sport
Belt	Fire	Murder	Sterilise
Bikes	Fix	Needle	Suicide
Blame	Flame	Overdose	Sunburn
Blood	Gas	Police	Swimming
Bong	Gloves	Pull	Tear
Break	Gun	Punch	Threaten
Care	Harm	Push	Trip
Cars	Hat	Putdown	Violence
Cigarette	Health	Rape	Water
Crime	Helmet	Right	Weapon
Cure	Help	Rip	Wrong

When talking about Safety issues there is always an aspect of A Fair Go involved. Therefore, the words in the Safety list could also be put under the Fair Go list because to bash, rape or murder someone isn't really giving them much of a fair go.

The lists are just to give you a hint as to which aspect to emphasise and therefore help you to sound as if you know what you're talking about. It seems that the older you get the easier it is to make a fool of yourself so it's always handy to have a little something to give you some confidence, especially when talking to super-intelligent kids about limits and rules.

Things to think about

✔ Making a distinction between right and wrong on an issue is forming a moral value.

✔ For parents to give moral guidance to their children they must know what their own moral values are.

✔ Adolescents' need for outside control is transferred from parents to their peer group as the first step towards passing control over to society in general and then to themselves in the form of self-control.

✔ 'It is wrong to deny people a fair go or to place people in any sort of danger' is a solid basis on which to make rules.

✔ It is handy to know the key words that indicate whether it is a fair go or safety that is the main concern in discussing a proposed rule.

CHAPTER 5

Parenting Style

S O FAR I HAVE concentrated mainly on child development. When I started this book I thought that would be the hard part over with but now I have to talk about parents and I find that parents are just as difficult to write about as kids. Probably because adults are just grown up kids. In other words, each parent has gone through the developmental stages we have been talking about that left them with a personality that is their own unique mixture of trust/distrust, autonomy/shame, purpose, competence and identity.

Parents also have their own mixture of logical thinking and moral judgement, along with their own idea of what is important in everyday life (values) and what is ultimately important (faith), be that spiritual or material.

Add to this the fact that parents are at a different stage of life to the kids and therefore have a whole set of new problems to solve, with no previous experience to help them. Parenting, the most difficult job on earth, is new to them and the only training there has been for this job is the example given by their own parents, who also had no training.

As if that isn't enough, I don't know if you are married, single, divorced or de facto. You may be part of a blended family made up of children from three past partnerships and your partner has just walked out. You may be just starting off in the job of being a parent or you may have six kids, one at each of the stages referred to in the previous chapters. You may have a violent or unco-operative partner or have a wonderful partner. You may not be a blood relation of any of the children in the family.

The days are gone when I can assume the family is a married couple with their own two and a half children. There are so many possibilities that I have to generalise by referring to you as 'the parent' and rely on you to adapt what you like from this to use in your own way. There are also so many possible combinations of people living together that I have to generalise and refer to the household as 'the family'.

The kids are not the only ones who have to change as they go through stages, so do the parents. At each stage of their development kids may go through a turmoil within themselves about getting what they want and making allowances for other people, as they learn the value of co-operation.

Parents go through a similar turmoil that is even harder and more complex because, unlike the children, the parent has a responsibility to cope with the demands and problems of many different stages all at once. There may be six children, one at each of the stages described, plus the stage of life of the parent, plus the partner's stage of life. As I said earlier, the most difficult job on earth. How many stages do you have to cope with?

Some kids seem to go through the different stages without any real problem and some parents seem to juggle the needs and wants and do their job without the turmoil within them causing any real problems but that doesn't mean the turmoil isn't there. The turmoil is there, sometimes very apparent, sometimes well under control, sometimes hidden very well.

Ideally, the parents start off having complete control over the children and gradually accustom them to the rules of life in such a way that the children eventually become self-controlled and repeat the process with their own children. To do this parents must gradually give over control of the children to the children and this is where conflict very often occurs.

The child may want this handover of control to happen much sooner than it should and the parent wants to delay it more than it should be delayed. On the other hand, the parent may be trying to get the child to take some control and the child is happier to have others make the decisions. Some parents say they want to keep control for the care and protection of the child, the child says the parent simply wants to control the child's life. These differences in outlook result in a great deal of trouble in families at adolescence.

The three parenting styles

We have so far considered six stages of childhood and three styles of discipline. Now I want to talk about the three styles of parenting that use the three ways to discipline children.

First there is the *dominant* parenting style that I will link with the extreme use of the intervention style of discipline. This is the parent who wants to 'own' the kids.

Second is the *smothering* parenting style that I will link with the extreme use of the interaction style of discipline. This is the parent who satisfies every whim of the child.

Third is the *permissive* parenting style that I will link with the extreme use of the non-intervention style of discipline. This is the parent who believes in allowing the kids to 'do their own thing' and doesn't set limits to behaviour.

The extreme use of any of the three parenting styles produce the same problem; unhappy, discouraged and irresponsible children. Of course there are many other things that can cause kids to be unhappy, discouraged and irresponsible but here we are only considering the parenting style.

As we will see later, every parent should use a mixture of all three parenting styles and at times should lean a little to one style more than the others, depending on the age of the child and the situation. However, some parents use one style most of the time and deserve the title of smothering, dominant or permissive.

The dominant parent

Parents who use the dominant parenting style most of the time will think parenting is a breeze when the kids are very little but life can be very dangerous for little children with parents who have a strong desire to control. The combination of a dominant parent and a belief in the use of violence to solve problems can lead to physical abuse and even death to a child if the child is difficult to control, especially if the child cries excessively or is at the tantrum throwing stage.

After the rebellion of the 2-two-year-old has been put down the dominant parent will quite rightly see the intervention style of discipline as the way to go for the 3-to-6-year-old because the child has settled again and is very conscious of the value of rules.

The age of reason comes along and with it the opportunity for having him join in the making of at least some rules but, because the child doesn't object, the dominant parent continues to make the rules. The primary school child's awareness of rules and belief in following them is certainly what is needed for the development of moral judgement and a dominant parenting style will certainly make him aware of rules. Because the parent makes the rules and uses force or threats of force to keep control, the child doesn't get practice at joining in the making of rules in order to develop that moral judgement.

The problem here is that instead of the child becoming aware of rules as being for sharing and caring, they are seen as being for winning and keeping control of others. Because of the parent's outlook on life, the constant daily message to the child is that force or violence is the way to win in the end and the time spent in front of the TV reinforces this outlook for the child.

Earlier I said that teenagers go through a conflict between the need for freedom and the need to belong. When the child reaches adolescence, parents who have managed to get away with a dominant style of parenting during the primary school years may be surprised at what seems like a change in character in the child.

The intervention style of discipline that was so effective for the preschooler can bring open rebellion to the parent still trying to use it on the adolescent. The child's physical size makes his need for freedom and his questioning of authority a threat to the dominant parenting style. Violence can erupt quite easily because the self-esteem of the parent may demand obedience from the child and the parent feels defeat if the child is allowed to 'win'.

The dominating parent demands that kids do exactly what they are told at all times and the parent can't cope with it if the child is being defiant or disobedient. The person acting from the desire to control a child cannot stand to have the child say 'no' and has to defeat the child or face what he sees as the humiliation of being defeated by a child.

This is why so many fathers have trouble coping with adolescent children. Men are socialised to be dominant and to be the problem solver of the family. When a man who has been socialised to be dominant and the problem solver for the family is faced with a defiant child, he is facing a situation where his whole self-esteem is on the line if he can't get this kid to do as he is told. Add to this the fact that force is the dominant person's ultimate problem solving tool and there is a potentially violent situation.

However, I find that when it comes to the discipline of children, women are only marginally behind men in the use of force or violence and the old method of, 'Wait until your father comes home' can be a cop-out for the woman who believes in violent solutions but doesn't want to be the one seen to do the job.

The smothering parent

The smothering parent uses the interaction discipline style to the extreme; she appears to put her own needs aside to give all to the child and indulges every whim of the children by trying to give them anything they want. She lavishes the children with love and attention and does everything for them. The kids never hear the word 'no' and never find out what it is like to wait for anything. Many of these parents believe that if they give the kids everything and make themselves indispensable to the children, the kids will be eternally grateful or at least be respectful to them.

These parents can become very disillusioned at the treatment they experience from children who have not developed the ability to see things from anyone else's perspective than their own. The kids remain self-centred and do not develop the concept of sharing and caring that comes from having to comply with the day-to-day rules of a household.

Smothering parents will make excuses for the negative behaviour of the children and protect them from the consequences of that behaviour. They find it almost impossible to discipline the kids even when they know that in the long run the children will be damaged by their way of parenting. This is strong evidence that the smothering or indulgent parent is thinking more of themselves than of the children. Their usual excuse for not disciplining the children is that, 'I love them too much to see them unhappy'.

Smothering parents complain loud and long about the emotional blackmail and disrespect they receive from the children and claim they don't deserve to be treated like that after all they have done for the children. Even in this they are only thinking of themselves.

The smothering parent would be horrified if accused of child abuse but the failure to discipline a child is a form of neglect and the neglect of a child is the abuse of a child. By not being assertive, the smothering parent fails to help a child develop an awareness of the value of rules for living by depriving the child of the necessity to make provision for the needs of others, thereby depriving the child of the very thing that helps develop moral judgement. This is neglect and abuse that will affect the child for life.

The smothering style or the dominant style can have the same effect. The smothering parent wants the child to always be dependent and prevents the child from becoming responsible and independent. The dominant parent tries to turn the child into exactly what the parent wants the child to be and prevents him from becoming responsible and independent. In other words, both parenting styles encourage dependence and irresponsible behaviour in the kids.

"IT'S ACE HAVING A SMOTHERING MUM."

The permissive parent

The permissive parent uses the non-intervention style of discipline for kids of all ages, even very young preschoolers, and believes kids should be allowed to 'freely express themselves'. They generally allow the kids to learn from experience and they seldom intervene to correct the child. These parents leave it to other people to let the child know his behaviour is obnoxious and then to put up with his abuse of their opinion.

Permissive parents may claim they are encouraging creativity in the child and allowing him to blossom forth in his own way but they do nothing to help the child channel that creativity.

Experience is certainly the best teacher but allowing a child to experience things he is not capable of handling is neglect and the same things said about the smothering parent's neglect can be said here.

Permissive parents will allow their children to watch what they like, read what they like, do what they like and say what they like. Unfortunately, when other people's kids are with their kids they will allow the same things for those kids, regardless of the age.

Many parents have commented on how the kids are quoting schools as teaching that parents cannot stop kids from doing whatever they want to do. To these kids, the term 'child abuse' has replaced 'open sesame' as the magic words opening all doors. One mother reported that her six year old claimed he would 'report her to Welfare' if she didn't buy him a drink.

This fear of being accused of child abuse may become fact through the parent failing to give the child appropriate discipline. The irresponsible teaching of rights to children is causing many children to be neglected in the very important area of moral and social development.

Responsible parenting

The responsible parent uses all three discipline styles for all ages of children. However, they alter the mix of those styles to suit the age or maturity of the child.

Preschool children at times have to be allowed to learn from experience (non-intervention), mainly when whatever they want to do isn't too harmful and they refuse to take direction. Preschool children should always be given an explanation about why they should or shouldn't do something and a chance to give an opinion (interaction). However, for the preschooler there should be more gentle but firm showing, teaching, directing, guiding, and telling than there is interaction or non-intervention.

Primary school children at times need to be gently but firmly directed, mainly when they refuse to consider the needs of others. School age children quite often need to learn from experience, especially in taking the consequences of their behaviour and at those times parents have to stand back and resist the temptation to save them. However, for the primary school age child there should be strong encouragement to join in making rules, if not at home then by getting them enrolled in team sports and other groups where they will learn the benefits of rules. Parents could encourage schools to engage kids in decision making on the rules of the school.

Adolescents certainly need parents who can use intervention at times to give firm guidance and direction, especially in what I have called stage one of adolescence, when their self-centredness causes others a problem.

Sometimes parents want teenagers to take notice of what they are told because the parents have made those same mistakes themselves and want to save the kids from those mistakes. The grandparents probably told the parents the same thing when they were adolescents but the parents went ahead and tried it for themselves anyway, because they had to learn from experience. Now their children are doing the same thing, taking no notice and making the same mistakes as their parents and their grandparents, because they want to learn from experience.

The interaction style of parenting that was of major importance for the primary school child remains an important part of the responsible parenting of teenagers because of the disputes over rules that seems to go hand in hand with having adolescents in the home.

Agreements on rules through the involvement of the kids in making those rules helps to bring peace to the home. There is no guarantee that agreed rules will bring peace when adolescents are involved but it is more likely.

However, the main parenting style to use with adolescents is an assertive non-intervention style. To stand back and allow the young adult to try new things, to make new friends, to take up new activities, to have successes, to make mistakes and to experience the consequences of those mistakes, but at the same time being assertive about the needs of all others in the house.

The non-intervening parent can give opinions and make statements about beliefs and values but makes no attempt to interfere and never says, 'I told you so'.

The non-intervening parent may state disapproval of the adolescent's behaviour and do nothing to encourage that behaviour but does not try to stop it and is very selective in stepping in to rescue the adolescent from the consequences of his behaviour.

Standing back and making no attempt to intervene can be extremely difficult for parents when a headstrong 13-year-old-girl refuses to take direction from them and is staying out all night drinking, smoking dope and tearing around in cars with 19-year-old-boys. Allowing her to take the consequences can also be extremely difficult.

Fortunately, most teenagers get through adolescence without doing those extreme things and it is much easier to allow them to have their way. Even those who become difficult usually settle down after a while and there are very few who continue to be irresponsible into adulthood.

The most fortunate parents are those who feel comfortable using all three parenting styles and can use which ever one they want to use at any given time, according to the particular child and the behaviour.

Parents and blaming

Parents are often faced with the expectations of some teachers, friends, relatives, police and others who think the parent is responsible for the behaviour of the child. I now want to explore this a little because when those same people are faced with their own children causing them a hassle, many of them start to blame everyone and everything except themselves as parents.

Most writers on parenting and most counsellors say that if parents want their children to change their behaviour, it is up to the parents to change their own behaviour first. Some of these writings even seem to suggest that the parents are to blame when their children break the law or suicide.

I also say that the parents must look at the way they treat the kids and to change their own behaviour if they want their children to change, but the difference is that I don't blame the parents for using the parenting methods they use. I don't believe that the parents are to blame for having the beliefs they have about what good parenting is. I believe that the parents are no more to blame for having their parenting style, than the kids are to blame for the way their parents treat them.

Too many people carry on the popular pastime of blaming the behaviour of the kids on the methods used by the parents. Parents are led to believe that they are to blame for having the beliefs they have about parenting, that they are to blame for using the discipline methods they use. Even the kids hang it on them sometimes, by saying things like, 'I didn't ask to be born. It's your job to control me'.

It isn't too long ago that parents were being encouraged to use punishments and rewards to 'shape' their children. It isn't that long ago that parents were being encouraged to let their children freely express themselves without any restrictions. It isn't that long ago that parents were being told to 'spare the rod and spoil the child'.

Small wonder that parents are a little suspicious of advice from 'experts' about parenting and small wonder that they cling to the methods they learned from their parents and from their own experience.

It seems to me that blaming the parents for the behaviour of their children is just another cop-out for people who don't want to accept responsibility for their own behaviour. They can always blame their own behaviour on the way they were treated as children and if they can get other people to accept this, then they have an excuse that can last a lifetime. And yet, there is a lot of truth in what they say.

The logical extension of blaming the parents is that the grandparents are then to blame for the behaviour of the parents. But this would also mean that the great-grandparents are to blame for the behaviour of the grandparents, and so on down the line. I am now a grandparent and hope to become a great-grandparent. From this way of looking at things, I am now to blame for the behaviour of my children, my grandchildren and my future great-grandchildren, and so on.

Does this mean that I am to blame if my great-grand-daughter robs a bank? This is a burden that's too heavy for me to carry so I'm going to try to get out of it and at the same time, hopefully, help you cope with this problem of parental responsibility.

When parents are to blame

If I had lived at the time of a man named Galileo, I would have believed that the earth was flat and all of my thinking and actions would be in line with that belief. I could not be blamed for having that belief, that was just the way it was. 'The earth is flat' was a belief that had been handed down always and it was a belief that I would have inherited. I could not be blamed for teaching my kids that the earth is flat because I would want them to know the truth as I knew it.

However, once I became aware of the convincing evidence about the earth being a globe that goes around the sun, and I ignored that evidence, I could be held responsible for holding the views I held about the shape of the earth.

To use another example, I have watched enough television to know that 'ignorance of the law is no excuse' and I believe that is a necessary attitude for the legal people to have. However, people should not condemn themselves or each other for doing harm they are genuinely unaware of. Once they are aware of the harm caused by their behaviour, it is a different thing. Once they are aware that their behaviour is causing harm to other people, and they continue to do it, they can be held responsible. They can also be held responsible for repairing the damage caused before they became aware of the effects of the behaviour, if possible, but they should not be expected to feel guilty about doing something they were not aware was doing harm.

A few years ago, my wife Rhonda and I were on holidays and we spent some time looking for things to take home to the kids, as well as sending postcards. As we were walking along the street Rhonda suddenly discovered that she had six cards in her hand that she had wandered out of the shop with and had not paid for.

We discussed what we were going to do about it, then headed back to the shop and told the shop assistant what had happened. Now, up to the point where Rhonda discovered she had the cards, she was only a little careless but to continue to walk in a direction away from the shop, knowing we had things that didn't belong to us, would make it hard to convince a magistrate that we intended to return the goods.

We are not to blame for believing the 'truths' that have been handed down to us, sometimes for generations, because we also believe them to be truths, but once we are aware that they are not really truths and we still hang onto them, we are responsible for holding them. This also applies to our parenting style, as much as some people will try to blame the parents for holding certain beliefs about parenting, those parents are only to blame for holding those beliefs if they become aware of a better way and still refuse to change to that way.

A woman came to me for help with her 15-year-old-son. He had become disobedient and untidy. His bedroom was a mess, he kept whatever hours he wanted and abused her when she tried to talk to him about his behaviour. He was a loner who had only one friend and couldn't make decisions for himself.

During our discussion, it soon became obvious that this woman had smothered the boy all his life and indulged his every wish. She believed her job as a mother was to meet the needs of her child and she had done this to the extreme. To her, she had done a good job of providing for him and she had kept him safe from the consequences of any silly behaviour.

It was during our second discussion that she became aware that she would have to change her treatment of her son if she wanted him to change, and part of what she would have to do would be to allow him to take the consequences of his own behaviour. She became aware that unless she disciplined him now, he could become even more irresponsible and be a very unhappy young man, who would continue that way through life.

We talked about different little things she could do to get practice at a new way but she could not bring herself to put him through any short term discomfort, it distressed her too much to see him suffer. At one stage she acknowledged that she was thinking more about herself than of him but she still could not do it.

Up to the point where this mother became aware of the harm her attitude was doing to her son she could not be 'blamed' for holding the views she held, but once she became aware of that harm she could be held responsible for doing harm and for doing nothing to repair past damage.

Another woman had the attitude that is typical of those who put up a barrier to change. She had two darling little daughters who gave everyone a hard time, except Mother. She turned a blind eye to the drinking, abuse and vandalising. It was the father who actually made the approach to me about the behaviour of his daughters. Mother reluctantly came along but only to tell me long and often that she loved the girls too much to discipline them. She couldn't bring herself to allow them to walk to school or get their own lunch and whenever anyone said anything to her along the lines of wanting her to make the kids a little more responsible for themselves she would simply reply, 'But I love my girls'.

Some will say that looking at parenting as an inherited thing gives parents an excuse for the way they act, allowing them a cop-out, that it isn't their fault they are saddled with a parenting method handed down for generations. That's not the case at all – quite the opposite. The parents of today are the ones who have been made aware of the finer points of child abuse, they are the ones who have had it pushed onto them to do something about some of the traditional parenting ways and who must face up to that responsibility for the sake of future generations. The reason it has to be seen as an inheritance is so the parents can look at it more objectively, as something they have that is beyond their control to have, but something that they have the responsibility to deal with.

Our beliefs and values as parents need to be examined

All of our ideas, values, beliefs have been given to us from our childhood, by direct teaching or by the example of other people. None of these beliefs or values are ours unless we look at them, examine them, compare them to other beliefs and values and then *decide* what we are going to do with them.

A wonderful thing about life is that we can have so much control over it by deciding what our own beliefs and values are. We can keep the ones that have been handed down. We can alter them and keep them. We can adopt some of the beliefs and values of other people and throw some of ours out. We can make these choices simply because the values and beliefs we carry around have been inherited or picked up and should be examined to see if we want to keep them.

Kids are not born with a prejudice towards other races, they are taught to hate. It is not really their belief until they examine it and decide to hate.

Most of our experimenting with beliefs and values was done at adolescence and once that turbulent time was over we tended to settle and generally stop this examination of attitudes. This is a shame because parenting generally misses out on this examination. Maybe it's because, at adolescence, actually parenting another person is not part of our experience except for being on the receiving end, and by the time we become parents we feel that the beliefs about parenting are ours. Besides, we are now busy, competent adults and can't admit to not being sure of ourselves. One mustn't be hesitant and unsure in this busy, busy world, must one?

I find it frustrating that even those who have been badly treated by their parents are still very likely to repeat that treatment of their own children, and say, 'That's how my parents did it and I turned out alright'. Even parents, who readily admit that they hated the way their parents treated them, continue to treat their own children in the same way.

Our beliefs and values are very personal and if someone questions them we tend to see it as an attack against ourselves. We may feel quite threatened and want to defend those beliefs and values. We feel we have to because in a sense we feel we *are* our beliefs and values. They form part of who we are and what we are, but is that identity something that has been pushed onto us or did we choose it?

Teenagers may seem to challenge all your values and beliefs but in fact they only challenge a few. When they challenge one it can be a shock to the system and you are faced with justifying a belief or value that you have just accepted and never examined before. This challenge can be seen as a disaster or as the teenager's contribution to the continuing development of the parent's thinking.

Things to think about

✔ Differences between parents and children about when parents hand over control of the child to the child cause a lot of trouble in many families, but this may be avoided by choosing appropriate parenting styles for each stage of the child's development.

✔ Stages of childhood, discipline styles and parenting styles go hand in hand for responsible parenting.

✔ Taking any style of parenting to extremes and using only one style of parenting can cause difficulties for both parents and children.

✔ It is important for parents to examine the beliefs, ideas and values which have been inherited or picked up from others to decide which of these they want to keep and use for their own parenting.

CHAPTER 6

Externalising the Rules

Controlling the parenting, not the child

I N PREVIOUS CHAPTERS we talked about the ideal situation of everyone concerned being involved in making the rules and limits. For most families this ideal is not very practical because many decisions have to be made on the spot and the parents have to make them. We also lumped all the worries, duties, fears, concerns, interests and so on under the headings of A Fair Go and Safety, to give you some tool to use in deciding the 'why' of a rule.

I have argued that an important reason for involving kids in decision making about rules is to assist the development of their moral thinking. Another reason for involving the kids is that it is important in solving the power struggle that causes so much trouble between parents and their teenage children.

Power struggles are the most common cause of relationship problems for parents and their adolescent children and power struggles are about rules and limits. There are many things that lead to disagreements and fights in a house but most of them are about ordinary things like how tidy the bedroom should be, about times to come home at night, and loud music. Sometimes, either as a worry or a reality, drugs, alcohol, sexual behaviour and 'hanging about the streets' is part of the time limits problem. Kids want more freedom than the parents are prepared to give, or think the kids are able to handle.

Usually power struggles have winners and losers, but when it comes to personal relationships, all are losers because of the resentments that are ever present, during and after a power struggle. The parent might get the child to give in but the child resents it and may resort to revenge to get even. On the other hand, if the child wins, the parent may try to lay on a heavy punishment in an attempt to regain control.

" *I THOUGHT IT WAS GOING TO BE ABOUT TEENAGERS..* "

Adolescence is a time when many parents believe they are losing their position as parents and one of the signs they see is the loss of the parental right to make the rules. They see any involvement of the kids in the making of rules as a weakening of their position as the parent. Their status is threatened by the loss of the absolute say in what the rules are going to be.

Others have little or no trust in their child's ability to make sensible contributions to rule making and point out the times rules have been agreed to and quickly broken.

This is a good reason why it is difficult for parents to genuinely share the rule making with their adolescents and why the parent's trust in the child's ability or willingness to take some responsibility for making the rules is seriously weakened.

There is no doubt that some kids will make agreements about rules and then break them almost as quickly as they make them. When they walk out of the room where they agreed to the new rule they walk into a different room with different people, and so the immediate situation is changed. The kids respond to immediate situations and the immediate situation is not the same as the one in which they agreed to the rule. This is quite understandable if you remember that they are so greatly influenced by what is happening right here and now.

Again I say that understanding a certain behaviour as being normal for that age does not mean that it should be accepted and allowed to continue. Understanding the behaviour allows parents to be a bit more gentle with the child while correcting the behaviour, without any hint of the behaviour being acceptable.

My experience with rebellious teenagers over the years has taught me that the more control we try to have over a child, the less influence we have on the child's behaviour. The more control we have over our parenting the more influence we have on the behaviour of the child. Therefore, to parents who want to have a feeling of 'being in control' I say shift your attention onto something you can get a great deal of control over – your own parenting.

Parents who manage to do this are able to cope with very difficult situations that previously would have them tearing their hair out. They abandon their attempts to directly control the child, assertively set the limits for themselves and the house, and generally gain more influence over the behaviour of the child.

What can make it very hard for parents is that a child may be refusing to take notice of the parents while at the same time insisting that they are responsible for controlling him.

Many parents have told me that when they stopped trying to control their children and made their children responsible for their own behaviour, they felt they had control of their parenting. How do you do this? There is no one easy way but from now on we will be looking bit by bit at gaining a feeling of being in control of your parenting situation.

The rules that need to be negotiated

What we will look at in this chapter is negotiating rules with teenagers but first I want to make it clear that I am not talking about negotiating all rules with the kids. If your home is running well in the way you do things, why upset it by introducing a new system? If the kids are happy with the rules there is no sense in causing problems. Take a leaf out of the TV repair man's handbook: if the television is running OK. don't try to fix it.

In the average home there are hundreds of rules. They are not noticed but they are there in the normal routine of the house, in the usual mealtimes, bed-times and where people sit at the table. There are unwritten rules about the order people use the bathroom, where the toothbrushes are kept, who reads the newspaper first, who sits in what chair in the lounge, who sleeps in what bed in which room, the language that is acceptable, which drawer is for the cutlery and many more little rules. People don't usually see them as rules, they see them as just the way things are done.

Changing your way of discipline for the children from using intervention for the preschooler to using interaction for the primary school child upwards does not mean sitting down and working out all the hundreds of rules with the kids. That would take forever and be totally unnecessary. The only rules that need to be negotiated are the rules that cause problems.

When compared to the number of rules there are in a home, kids who are difficult to manage only break a few, even though it seems as if they 'break all the rules'. Probably they would break four or five of the hundreds of rules that exist and it is only these rules that need to be negotiated.

Negotiating boundaries, limits and rules

The difference between boundaries, limits and rules

The words 'Limits', 'Rules' and 'Boundaries' are generally used to mean the same thing. However, I want to make a distinction between the three to explain the idea of giving kids a sense of having freedom of choice. For this purpose *boundaries* set out an area, *limits* allow people to make decisions about what activities they want to do in that area and *rules* are specific and definite about what is acceptable behaviour in that activity. Believe it or not, boundaries, limits and rules can be very positive, challenging, exciting and acceptable to teen-agers. They can also be frightening so that they want to stay a little close in case things get out of hand.

Maybe an example will help the explanation. With little kids parents say, 'Go out in the backyard and play cricket and make sure it's fair for everyone by keeping to the rules'. The backyard is the boundary, playing cricket and being fair are the limits and the rules are the rules of cricket.

At other times, parents remove all dangerous material from the backyard, those who are lucky enough to have a yard, leave the kids in there and confidently allow them to decide for themselves what to do for amusement. The limit to them making rules is set by, 'Make sure you make up games that everyone can play'.

In this way, the conditions are set for the kids to decide for themselves what they are going to do to amuse themselves. When parents do this they are setting the conditions that encourage a child to develop a sense of safety in making decisions and a sense of freedom of choice within limits. The kids are happy because they feel both safe and free and the parents are happy because the kids are safely out of their hair for a little while. Still using this example, the more decisions the parents make about what and how the kids can play increases the time the parent has to remain in the backyard to make sure the kids stick to the rules.

Parents may not have been aware of it but in providing areas for free play they were encouraging the kids to make decisions and take control of their own lives. Those same principles that were involved in the backyard example of the early years can also be used for the teenage years, with some adjustments to suit the changed circumstances. The greatest change is that the child has grown and needs wider boundaries.

This is similar to the changed physical need for bigger clothing; it would be ridiculous to try to fit your large teenager into the clothing she wore as a 2-year-old. She may still act like a 2-year-old at times but her clothing has to match her physical size, not her behaviour.

Teenagers are no different to little children when it comes to needing boundaries or fences to see what parts of their lives they control and their area of freedom in making decisions about what to do. A major difference about teenage boundaries is that they can't be seen as easily as a fence.

What are the boundaries of a child's life? There is the education area, the home area, the social area, the occupation area, the time filling area, the entertainment area and the religious area.

An example of a boundary can be, 'Each person can make their own decisions about their own education'. An example of a limit to that freedom can be, 'As long as that decision does not affect other people'. An example of a rule would then be, 'Any decision to be made about education that affects another person must be talked over with that person before the decision is made'.

Boundaries and limits form the security blanket that we all need, so we know how far we can go in making decisions. Adults come to accept that they only have freedom to make decisions within limits and they generally see that this is the way it has to be for society to work. Even though adults sometimes break a limit, they would still believe in the need for the limit to be there.

The above also applies to teenagers, except that some will not want to admit the necessity for boundaries or limits. It's much the same with rules; teenagers in general are well aware of the need for rules and don't want to do away with all rules. There are a few that they are unhappy about and it is these few rules that cause all the trouble.

Sometimes the young person will go to an extreme in trying to shake conditions he sees as too restrictive. Some just don't see the need for restrictions to be there and any limit or rule imposed by the parent simply leads to another fight in the power struggle.

The great need for freedom is to *feel* free and this feeling can occur even within strict limits. However, always remember that regardless of whether the limits are narrow or wide, kids will still test them.

Teenagers argue for the here and now

The chapters on child development indicate that a natural, normal and extremely annoying aspect of negotiating limits with adolescents is the trouble they have seeing past what they want to do now, and they will argue endlessly to be able to do what they want to do right now.

When it comes to deciding on rules, the meaning of 'negotiated' is closer to 'discussion' and far removed from 'argue'.

Unions should all employ 13-year-olds to do their negotiating for them because of their ability to argue in protecting past gains and pushing hard for new ones. This ability leads people to say, 'He is 13 going on 25' when in fact the way he is arguing and the extent of the logic used really means that he is simply 13 going on 14.

I believe arguing at length with a teenager delays their development because arguing can cement a person into their present opinion; certainly discuss things at length but don't waste time arguing.

When the parent is the rule maker and sets the limits there are usually many arguments and the teenager can start to 'nitpick' and set traps for the parent. One way they do this is to say that unless the parent actually said 'no' to something then it implied that it was OK to do it. But if the parent does say a straight out 'no' the teenager then has something to openly argue at length about, or to openly defy, or to say, 'See, you're always trying to tell me what to do'.

There are kids who will do anything to get out of being a part of making rules because they then feel a pressure to keep to those rules when what they really want is to do whatever they feel like doing at the time. They want the parents to be the one to make the rule even though they complain bitterly about that and if they do make their own rules they generally break them anyway.

Non-negotiable limits and rules

There are some rules and limits that are not open to negotiation, such as law-breaking behaviour. There may be other limits and rules that you have for your home that you consider serious enough to be non-negotiable because of religious or cultural reasons or because you have to cope with a child or person who has special needs.

Parents must be prepared to stick to whatever the rules are if they want to give their children a high level of respect for rules and limits. Parents and caregivers must 'practise what they preach' because the kids will follow their example, not their words. Double standards can be confusing to kids and undermine their respect for rules.

Example is the main teacher of values, therefore it is extremely important for the parents to stick to the limits – the non-negotiable ones and the negotiated ones.

Alright, it's time to start talking about how to negotiate the boundaries, limits and rules that are causing a dispute in the home. There are some general rules about negotiation that may help in working out all sorts of problems with all sorts of people. The first of these rules is to separate the people from the problem.

General guidelines about negotiation

We said above that the only rules that need to be negotiated are the rules that are causing problems and disputes. Disputes usually occur over rules being broken but an over-compliant child or dependent child can also be a problem. The problem may be that the child relies too much on other people to make decisions for him.

The anger and frustration of trying to be the rule maker can be avoided by putting the responsibility back onto the teenager to come up with a rule that will give everyone involved a fair go and be safe. The parent can be as cheerful and agreeable as they like, while simply stating that as long as A Fair Go and Safety aspects are met, fine, the rule is that you can have a new rule.

So there may be a need to negotiate because a child needs to be held back a little or because a child needs to take more responsibility than he wants to. Either way, the guidelines for negotiating are the same.

Separating the people from the problem and the rules

In football terms this would mean playing the ball and not the man. This sounds easy enough but in practice it is difficult to do because we tend to see the people as the problem instead of seeing people as having a problem. We try to change the people instead of working on the problem itself.

A difficult part of separating the people from the problem is for the parent to stop seeing the problem as theirs to fix because, generally, problems in a family start off belonging to one person but quickly become family problems. In a later chapter we will look at deciding who owns any particular problem, what is important here is the feeling of resentment towards the other person when a problem exists. The parent may feel angry towards the child because there is a problem with time limits and the child may feel angry with the parent because there is a problem with time limits. What I want to do is switch the attention onto the problem (time limits) and away from the people.

The problem is the time limits, not the people. Something about the time limits needs to be sorted out, not the people. A complication for some of us as parents is that most of the rules are made by us and are part of our value system. Because our values are a part of us and form what we are, we see disagreement with our rules as being disagreement with us as parents and as people. However, the fact is that because we made the rule for a good reason at some time in the past, we can also unmake the rule for a good reason.

The good reason is that there is a dispute over the time limits and we can take the opportunity to give the kids some experience at making up new time limits that suit everyone concerned, including the parents. For those who are concerned about losing parental control there is no loss of parental control, just a shift in how that control is exercised. Again the shift is towards controlling the parenting rather than controlling the kids.

Seeing the problems as separate from the people involved means seeing our rules as just being solutions to past problems, solutions that may no longer fit the new problems. The rules become objects that can be discussed to try to find a better way for the family to work. This can be difficult because we get security from our rules and it takes some courage to decide to allow other people, especially kids, to have a large say in the rules.

All this is called 'externalising the rules' and means that the problem rules are no longer the parent's rules but become the responsibility of everyone who contributes to them. Rules, limits and boundaries become something that can be judged for their effect on people and things without anyone feeling they have to defend the rules and limits as being a part of themselves.

For step parents and blended families, this externalising of rules is even more important. The added difficulties of bringing together people who have lived by different rules makes it so much more important to separate those people from their rules, so that the judgement of their rules isn't a judgement of them as people.

Some families decide to write down any new rules and this is actually a good way to externalise the rules. Other families believe they don't need written rules but this doesn't mean that they can't refer to agreements they make as being 'The Rules', or 'The Guidelines' or whatever terms they want to use. An unwritten constitution can still help every person in the house feel they belong, by having something to discuss, and maybe to sometimes have a healthy 'bunfight' about.

Keep in mind that we are generally only talking about a few rules but when those few rules are negotiated fairly, members feel that 'The Rules' belong to them all and no one member alone has the power to make them. One of the great advantages of this is that the strain of running things, or the blame for things going wrong, doesn't rest on any one person.

When 'The Rules' exist and a child wants to do something, all the parent has to say is, 'What was the rule about that?' She doesn't have to take the role of the ruler laying down the law but can take the role of someone helping the child to make, interpret, remember and keep to agreements that are made through considering the needs of everyone involved.

Remember, a problem is only a problem until a solution is found and the solution does exist. Included in this is the problem of separating yourself from your rules.

Negotiating from 'the needs', not from 'the solution'

Usually when we start negotiating with someone we already know our solution to the problem and that's how we think it should be done. We then argue for our solution to be adopted by the other person. We feel that if the other person doesn't accept our solution we are being rejected. Unfortunately the other person has also decided how it should be done and his solution will solve the problem from his point of view.

Because rules are solutions to problems you may think the above is only repeating what was said in the last section and to some extent it is. The difference is that we are now talking about what is left after people are separated from the problem (from the rule). What is left are the needs and wants that led to that rule or solution being decided on in the first place. It was a good rule and it served a purpose. What was that purpose? When you know why the rule was made you can judge whether any suggested rule solves the same problem as good as, or better than, the old rule.

Every person affected by the problem, say time limits, will look at it from their own point of view and will probably have their opinion on a solution to that problem. A teenager will decide that he wants the time limit to be 4 a.m. and the parent will want the time limit to be 10 p.m. Each will argue for their time limit to be accepted and as they argue they dig a hole for themselves about the time limit, a hole so deep that they cannot climb out.

The teenager's solution to his needs doesn't suit the parent and the parent's solution to her needs doesn't suit the teenager. What I am proposing is that both listen to and talk about each other's needs, and try to find a new solution that each can live with. There is always more than one way to solve a problem and maybe one of the unthought of and untried solutions will be acceptable to both. The mere willingness to attempt to find a workable solution that is acceptable to both teenager and parent helps the relationship because there is respect for the needs of the other person.

Some parents will find it extremely difficult to make sure their own needs are met in any negotiation over rules if the kids use trickery, blackmail, fear, emotional pressure, sympathy, or guilt to gain the advantage. Other parents will use all those same things to gain the advantage over the kids. Real problems occur when the parent and the kids are using those strategies on each other.

Some parents will have to deal with kids who are aggressive in wanting their own way without considering other people, or they may have to deal with kids who submit too easily and encourage them to stick up for themselves. On the other hand, some parents will be too aggressive in pushing their own views and some will be too submissive and give in to what the kids want.

The ideal outlook for parents to have in negotiating problem rules is assertiveness, something we will discuss in the next chapter.

Having rules about making rules

One of the first things to talk about in negotiating new rules to replace the few problem rules is a set of rules about how to change rules. The question, 'What is the rule about that?' can be helpful in putting responsibility for the rules on to the children. The same applies when a child claims a rule should be changed, 'You say you broke the rule because you are unhappy with it. What did we agree was the way to go about having a rule changed?'

Putting the responsibility back to the child often reveals that the child avoided the process because of something he wanted there and then and could not have if he went by the rule. This may mean there is no need to change the rule but, hopefully, there would be a consequence that would apply in such a situation.

In the chapter on moral judgement I lumped all needs, concerns, worries, duties and wants under the headings of Safety and A Fair Go. That was con-

" JUST A MOMENT CAMERON - DON'T WE HAVE A RULE ABOUT THAT ? "

venient then and is convenient again here so I can suggest a rule about making or changing rules. One rule about changing rules could be that if a new rule could be thought up that met the safety and fair go aspects at least as well as the old rule did then there is no problem in having the new rule.

Having a rule that any new rule must consider the needs of everyone involved provides parents with a tool for teaching their children about caring and sharing and takes the heat off themselves because they no longer have to think up and impose rules.

When a child whinges and nags about a rule, simply ask him what he thinks the rule was made for, listen to his answer and add other Fair Go and Safety aspects he hadn't mentioned, if any. Then tell him if he can come up with a plan to do what he wants to do, fine, but it must be liveable for everybody involved or the old rule applies.

Wouldn't it be a wonderful change to have the kids being the ones to have to think about the needs of everyone before trying to get a rule changed to suit themselves.

Usually parents become angry and frustrated with the continual pressure from a child nagging for a rule to be changed but at least the nagging means he recognizes you as the person he needs approval from. He wants to do something and needs your approval to do it, that's why he wants you to be the one to change the rule. The problem is that many teenagers want rules that will follow their constantly changing wants; in other words they want a set of rules designed especially for them.

A final rule about changing rules could be that new rules have to be within the law. Sometimes a solution may seem logical and the parent has no personal problem with it but it is illegal and cannot be agreed to if respect for rules is part of what the parent is trying to instil in the kids.

The parental 'Duty of Care'

Parents are members of the household and any rule has to allow for the fair go and safety of all members of the household. One of the Fair Go aspects that has to be taken into account when making up a rule is the 'duty of care' responsibility of the parent, which is something not only felt by the parent but required by law, and carries a penalty if the parent neglects that duty. The parent's duty to provide care and protection for the child is often seen by the teenager as the parent simply wanting to have control.

Sometimes the parent's duty of care means making sure the kids are aware of the consequences of their behaviour but as we saw in the chapters on development, kids have difficulty seeing far into the future and will generally disregard any consequence that is not immediate. Parents become very frustrated trying to convince children of the dangerous consequences of their behaviour and feel they might as well talk to the trees.

The effect of some behaviours may not occur until years later, giving the impression that there is no bad effect at all. Sexually transmitted diseases and smoking are examples where the effects can take years to become apparent.

A rule about this could be that as much information as possible has to be gathered about health issues or dangerous behaviour to avoid disagreements through ignorance. In many instances the parent has met the duty of care by making sure the kids are aware of consequences and can do no more because the kids insist on continuing with the behaviour.

Helping kids think up new rules

There is always more than one way of solving a problem. Once the needs of those involved are known and it's agreed that any new rule must be liveable for everyone, there is no reason why you can't join in and help the kids think up ways they can have what they want.

Every suggestion can be listened to and discussed in the light of the set conditions. There will probably be some weird and wonderful arguments put to support some suggestions and the parent may have to do three things at once. One, restrain from rubbishing suggestions. Two, protect the interests of the 'weaker' members of the family. Three, protect your own interests.

The aim of thinking up alternatives is to find one that everyone accepts as liveable. That doesn't mean that everyone has to completely agree with it but they can be reasonably at ease with it.

Know what you intend to do if negotiation doesn't work

One of the great advantages kids have when they negotiate with parents is that they know what they intend to do if the negotiation doesn't go their way. For instance, a child trying to get permission to stay out late may have already decided to 'fall asleep at a mate's place' if the permission is not given.

Parents can learn from the kids in this regard. Whenever you are going to approach a child to negotiate something, decide beforehand what you are going to do if the child refuses to discuss it or the negotiation fails in some way. For instance, you have tried to talk to the child about doing his washing but he is not very talkative. 'Alright, I can see that we are not going to come to an agreement over this so I will wash clothes that are put in the laundry basket and only the clothes in the laundry basket. Any clothing I have to pick up will be put on your bed, unwashed. Let me know if you want to talk about changing any of this.'

Deciding what you are going to do beforehand gives you a good deal of control over the situation and helps to avoid the frustration of trying to work things out with someone who is refusing to talk, or being difficult about it. There is no need to get upset because you already know what you intend to do.

The important thing to remember is that whatever you intend to do has to be under your control and not something that can be defied. For instance, it's no good deciding to send a 15-year-old to his room if he doesn't co-operate because he can refuse, then what do you do? No, the things that are under your control are the things that you are going to do or not do. In other words, co-operation goes both ways and you can state what you want in return for your co-operation or you can state what you are not going to do.

Things to think about

✔ Power struggles about rules and limits are the most common cause of relationship problems between adolescent children and parents.

✔ The more control parents try to have over the child the less real influence they may have on the child's behaviour.

✔ Parents who want to feel in control and have influence on their teenager's behaviour can shift their attention to controlling their own parenting rather than the teenager.

✔ Boundaries, limits and rules, negotiated by parents and children, allow children to make decisions, feel safe and free, and learn to be co-operative and responsible.

✔ Negotiate from the needs of the parent and the child rather than the pre-determined solution each may have in mind.

✔ Parents need to have a back-up position if the child refuses to negotiate or the negotiation fails.

✔ A problem is only a problem until a solution is found, and a solution does exist!

CHAPTER 7

Assertiveness

What it means

BEING ASSERTIVE is what most of this book is all about. Being assertive basically means sticking up for your right to safety and a fair go without violating the rights of others to safety and a fair go. Having respect for your own needs and wants and respect for the needs and wants of other people.

Some parents consider only themselves and the kids have to fit in. They own the kids and never consider them in any decisions that affect the child's life. This can range from parents making big decisions like changing towns and schools to everyday decisions like imposing time limits centred on the parent's own social needs.

At the other extreme are the parents who sacrifice their own needs to meet the needs of the kids. They put aside their own social and educational needs and become slaves to the needs of the kids.

By learning to be assertive parents find a balance between their own needs and the needs of the kids. Deliberately sticking up for yourself with small things and at the same time considering the needs of the kids is the best way to learn to be assertive. You can do this with everybody, not just with the kids.

The things that are not worth making a fuss about are the very things that can provide you with the easiest and most frequent way to practise being assertive. The fact that these things are not worth making a fuss about results at one extreme in parents not bothering to consult the kids and at the other extreme in parents giving in to the kids. Parents at both ends miss out on learning to be assertive about something worthwhile when it occurs. Being assertive with kids means sometimes saying 'no' to them and the easiest way to practise this is in small things that you don't want them to have.

The rights of adults

Many parents at our parenting nights have expressed surprise that they have the right to say 'no' to their kids. Others have been surprised that they have the right to set some rules for their house. The first time I heard parents say these things I thought they were joking but I've heard it many times since.

The most important thing about rights is that unless you know what your rights are, you have no way of knowing when your rights have been abused and you don't know what you can be assertive about. You didn't think adults had rights?

I came across this list of adult rights and I think they should be known by every parent who has been made feel guilty for having needs and wants.

As a human being you have the right to:

1 Set your own goals and make your own decisions.

2 Be treated with respect.

3 To have and express your own opinions and feelings.

4 Say 'NO' to requests.

5 Ask for what you want.

6 Make mistakes.

7 Choose to behave assertively.

8 Choose NOT to assert yourself.

9 Change your mind.

10 Take time to slow down and think.

How many of these rights do you actually exercise? If you don't exercise a right, you don't really have it.

" WOW - YOUR MUM GAVE YOU A REAL TONGUE-LASHING. "
" YEAH ... IT MUST BE WORTH A FEW 'FREQUENT-FLAYER-
POINTS ... "

When to be assertive

The Serenity Prayer

Lord, grant me the serenity to accept that which I cannot change. Grant me the courage to change that which I can change and grant me the wisdom to know the difference.

I can't give you the serenity to accept the things you can't change. Neither can I give you the courage to change the things you can change but I can be God's little helper and give you a guide in how to know the difference. Then, if you want to, you can use that knowledge to gain the strength to change things or to get the serenity to accept things, but that's up to you because miracles are outside my powers.

To practise accepting what you cannot change and changing what you can change, you must know the difference.

When a child is born, the parent rightly believes that the child's problems are the parent's responsibility to solve. When baby is uncomfortable, you change her nappy. When she is hungry, you feed her, and so on and on. It becomes a part of being the parent that as soon as the child lets you know of a problem you accept that it is your responsibility to solve it and this is one of the great strengths of parents in establishing a relationship with the child.

As will be discussed in a later chapter, our greatest strengths are also our greatest weaknesses. There can come a time when believing the child's problems are your problems can be used against you in a power struggle or it can be used by a child to avoid responsibility. It can also be used by you to try to hang on to control of the child long after control should have been handed over to the child, or it can result in you feeling you are a failure because you can no longer solve the child's problems.

The baby is so helpless for so long that some parents could be said to become addicted to the child's problems. For these parents to 'kick the habit' of doing everything for the child brings physical signs of distress. They can feel so bad that they give in and solve the kid's problems, even when they know they are preventing the child from becoming an independent adult.

Whose problem is it?

What a parent can become assertive about is who is responsible for solving the problems that come along but to do this you have to be able to decide quickly what you can change and what you can't. The first step in the answer to the Serenity Prayer is to have a way of knowing who *initially* owns the problem.

The person who does the approaching is the person who initially owns the problem. To decide whether you want to accept ownership of the problem or share ownership or leave ownership with the one who did the approaching, I suggest that you quietly ask yourself two questions before deciding how to handle the situation.

1 Who made the approach about it?

2 Do I want (to) help?

This is not a new idea, kids seem to instinctively know all about this and it can be maddening when an adult approaches them about something and the kid says, 'Well, why tell me? It's your problem, not mine'.

It seems that at the birth of the first child, as the baby is handed to the parent, this knowledge of who owns problems is removed from the parent's brain. When the parent accepts responsibility for the child, some do it totally and permanently instead of accepting it only in proportion to the child's level of dependence.

Many parents think that it is their responsibility to be warning their children of any problems that lie ahead of them. Or always telling them the likely consequences of what they are doing. Many parents are amazed when told that they can allow their children to discover the bad consequences for themselves sometimes. That as long as there is no real danger, let them learn for themselves, especially if they become annoyed with you when you tell them what the likely outcome will be.

Sometimes when I'm approaching a child I find it difficult to see why it's my problem because most of the time I'm approaching about something I believe the child is doing wrong. This opens up a lot of questions that I have to ask myself: Just what is my problem? Why am I approaching this kid? Just how is the behaviour affecting me? What am I complaining about? Am I worried about something that might happen? Is it a behaviour the kid should be modifying? Who says so? Is it just a standard of mine that I'm forcing on the kid?

'But surely I don't have to solve all my own problems', you say, 'Why can't I ask others to help?' Accepting that it's your problem doesn't mean you can't ask others to help. Getting other people to help is a responsible way to solve problems.

The main point of the question, 'Do I want (to) help?' is to remind me that I probably want the child's co-operation in solving my problem. Maybe I'm approaching him about the rotten mess in his bedroom and I want it cleaned up. How I approach him about it is what is important because I'm sure that if I use the words 'rotten mess' I'll only get into an argument.

Once I have worked out what it is that I'm unhappy or concerned about I can use statements starting with 'I' to acknowledge that I know it's my problem. For example, 'I don't want you to ride the bike without a light because you might get hurt' is far less likely to end in a fight than, 'I'm telling you not to ride that bike without a light'. Orders or demands that start with 'I' are not 'I' statements, they are just orders and demands.

When someone approaches me with a problem, I can use the word 'You' to let him know that I'm aware it's his problem and it doesn't become mine unless, or until, I accept it. 'Do I want to help?' Yes, up to a point. Although it's still his problem, maybe I will decide to accept part ownership of it and offer my help to share in solving the problem.

For this to work well, 'The Problem' has to be seen as something separate to the person. The child isn't the problem, the child has a problem. The parent isn't the problem, the parent has a problem. Problems can usually be solved quickly when the *appropriate* person or people accept responsibility for solving it. The difficulty is to get the owners to admit or accept ownership.

So it's possible to look at this problem business in much the same way as we have looked at the parenting style that we inherited and some of the rules. We can externalise problems and see them as separate to ourselves. It may be my problem but I am not the problem, I am someone who has a problem. Once I get rid of that problem I will be the same person I was before but will no longer have the problem.

Looking at the ownership of problems this way doesn't only apply to kids, you can use it whenever anyone approaches you with a problem, to decide what problems you want to reject, what problems you want to share with the person carrying the problem, and what problems you want to take on as your own.

To put it the other way around, when I am the one doing the approaching, it allows me a way of deciding which problems I'm just stating as a problem of mine, which ones I'm wanting the other person to help me with, and which problems I'm wanting the other person to take off my hands and accept as her own.

Some people may think this is a cold and uncaring attitude to problems—too matter of fact and definite. I believe that it is in fact a very caring attitude and can be more effective in helping people. Uncertainty causes so many people to become confused and frustrated trying to solve problems that they have no hope of solving, and missing out on recognizing the ones they could have solved.

Having a clear-cut method of deciding who initially owns what problem can give you a peace of mind and a clear view of things that helps you to work on getting the serenity to accept the situation as it is and the courage to do what you can do.

You cannot solve the problems of kids or anyone else unless they let you solve them and your life can be made miserable by someone constantly handing you problems to solve and then doing everything to obstruct you as you try to solve them. A person can control you and your happiness, or should I say your misery and frustration, and leave you feeling a helpless failure. This situation is very common between parents and teenage children.

Using 'I' statements and 'You' statements are the assertive way of letting kids know who initially owns the problem and the use of 'We' statements (or combining 'Me' and 'You' in a statement) is the assertive way of letting them know of your wish to share the problem.

How 'The Approach' can be used to boost self-esteem

You have power over your child's level of self-esteem whenever he approaches you about anything and whenever we have power over another person there are always those people who will deliberately use it to keep the upper hand. However, I believe most want to help their children by raising their self-esteem.

Let's imagine we are watching a video tape of your child approaching you about a problem and we use the slow motion button to get to the point where the actual first contact is made, probably using the familiar one word question, 'Mum?'. Now hold the picture at that point.

I stopped the tape before your response because this is the point at which you have control over the self-esteem of your child. How you respond can either raise or lower the kid's self-esteem, can either build her up or push her down, can either encourage her or crush her, can boost confidence or damage it for life. With power like that, I think we will leave the tape paused for a moment so you can think about how you're going to respond.

What you first feel like doing will depend on your feelings and your own problems, and these are obviously important, but the child is not aware of your problems and will take your response as a judgement about herself and the importance you place on her. As I have said many times, kids are naturally highly self-centred and will only alter over time. It's just the way things are with them. That self-centredness is a real handicap that works against them as they may see every action of other people as a judgement of themselves.

If their first approach to you results in a put down of some kind, a child with a high level of self-esteem may be willing to risk some of it by approaching you a second time, because he still has some in reserve. However, a kid with low self-esteem, who loses some in the first approach, is not so likely to risk losing any more by making the second approach to you.

Some kids are lucky enough to have one or two good 'Self-Esteem Service Stations' (friends, relations who give her a boost) to call on for repairs but if you are the only Self-Esteem Service Station the child has, where does she go to for repairs if you damage it?

Alright, now that you know how much power you have over your child's self-esteem, you can start the tape again whenever you're ready.

You can accept the problem the child has approached you about, you can leave it for the child to solve or you can offer assistance by sharing the problem. As far as self-esteem is concerned, it doesn't matter what your decision is about ownership of the problem, it only matters how you put your decision across. In other words, there is a difference between *how* you respond and *what* your response is. The 'what' is important but the 'how' is even more important.

It isn't just the words that are important in the response; there is also the emphasis put on different words. And what about the non-verbal ways you use to show how you feel. All these things will be noticed by the super-sensitive child and will be taken personally, simply because that's the way kids are.

You can leave the young person with the problem and do it in a way that boosts her up: 'I have complete confidence in you being able to solve that and I will support you no matter what your decision is'. You can relieve the child of the problem but do it in a way that damages her; 'Yes, I'll do it for you because you would only mess it up as usual anyway'.

Just before we get off the topic of the power you have over the one doing the approaching, I want to point out that the opposite is also true. Every time you approach someone else you put that high level of power into the hands of the person you approach. This is one of the reasons it is important to use the right approach or take the consequences of the risk you take.

'I' statements are a way of reducing the amount of self-esteem you lay on the table when you approach someone. You may decide to risk a bit more by asking for help or you may decide to just present the problem as yours and leave it up to the other person to offer to help.

Either way, you can know and feel that you are in control of your situation and gain strength from that. How the other person responds to you then reflects on them, not on you, just as how you respond to others reflects on you.

Some problems need to be uncovered by a third person

Even parents and kids who normally get along very well can come into conflict about something and not be able to work it out because the real problem is hidden. Quite often the teenager identifies the problem but can't, or won't, tell the parent about it and starts to 'act out'.

Time and time again, the teenager will know deep down what the problem is but they find it too difficult to voice it at first. They want a good relationship with the parent and fear that if they voice their problem that relationship will be damaged and the parent hurt.

The parent also wants a good relationship but, in general, has not looked at that relationship except as a parent/child status relationship.

In a mediation session, we were exploring the conflict from a 13-year-old-girl not washing the dishes when she was told to and in general being defiant

"I SENSE THAT YOU HAVE A PROBLEM, CAMERON."

towards her mother. On one occasion the daughter had run away after an argument about washing the dishes and at other times the mother had resorted to hitting her. The hitting had also resulted in the daughter running away.

One of the great things about mediation is that it is probably the first time each person in the conflict has had a chance to say what they want to say without interruption and it is probably the first time each has listened without interrupting. After each had this opportunity we reached the point where it became obvious to both that the daughter, to use her words, felt 'like shit' when her mother ordered her around and the mother felt like a worthless failure when the daughter defied her. Both wanted to be treated with respect but up to now the daughter could only express that by rebellion and the mother could only see the rebellion as the daughter's rejection of her as a mother.

By her rebellion, the daughter was really trying to tell her mother, 'You can't make me do anything, so start treating me more as an adult. I know I still need a lot of guidance and support but I am entitled to be treated with respect'.

The mother came to the point where, 'I realise now that you are nearly an adult. I can still give you support and guidance but I need to be treated with respect as I do that'.

The rest of the mediation was spent discussing ways they could both have what they needed from each other while still maintaining the mother/daughter relationship. Washing the dishes was not the real trouble and it became clear that the daughter believed she should take her turn at the dishes and didn't want anything changed as far as responsibilities were concerned.

This reminded me that many of the 'uncontrollable' young people we worked with saw our house rules as reasonable even though those rules were very similar to the rules they had rebelled against at home. It was not the rules themselves that caused the problem but how the child felt about the way those rules were either devised or imposed.

Assertiveness: questions and statements

Listening

There are only two points I want to make about listening. Firstly, one of the reasons we don't hear what others are saying is because we are too busy thinking about what we want to say as soon as we get the chance. Most of the time we miss what's really being said because we are impatiently waiting for them to shut up so we can say something we think is important.

You cannot pay attention to two things at the same time. To hear what someone is saying, pay attention to what she is saying and not have your mind on what to say next.

Take note of how often you are just waiting for someone to stop talking so you can say something. Did you really hear what he said? If you want to practise something about listening, practise putting thoughts out of your head until the other person has finished speaking and you will become a good listener.

Secondly, being a good listener doesn't help with the teenagers who seem to believe that the arguments that go on in their head are known by the people around them.

Example

One young woman complained about her mother ignoring her needs when she had told her she needed space. It turned out that in her mind she had told Mum through non-verbals like staying in her room brooding and by not eating with the rest of the family. She assumed that her mother would know she was brooding and would put the same meaning to those things as she did.

Having the power to read minds could also be an advantage to parents at times.

Example

One girl claimed that her mother was always yelling at her, although the mother denied ever yelling at her. One day when I was talking to the two of them, the girl declared, 'See, she's yelling again'. The mother had not raised her voice but had started criticising the girl. Further talking revealed that the 'yelling' the girl referred to was when the mother criticised her in some way.

Therefore, 'listening' can mean taking notice of actions and words together and trying to understand the underlying message as kids respond to questions and statements.

Questions

Many parents find that every time they try to tell a young person something, he already knows it but when they want to find out something from the child he knows nothing. Amazing!

Questions are wonderful tools of communication and we can't do without them but, like all tools, they can be deliberately used to do good or harm. Questions in games like Trivial Pursuit can be fun things, but in other situations, such as talking to survivors of sexual abuse, careless questions can cause great pain.

A child's self-esteem can be damaged by the sort of questions she is asked, but questions can also build up a child's self-esteem. Questions which, from the child's point of view, seem to accuse or blame or belittle can lower their self-esteem. And questions that frustrate them or cause them to become defensive can lead into power struggles and resentment, as well as causing a lowering of their self-confidence. All this negativity could be an explanation for the dislike kids have for questions and why they rely so much on mumbling, 'Dunno' to so many questions.

Putting an insult into the question adds a sharp edge to the cutting power of the question. 'Why did you do a stupid thing like that, you idiot?' is not the sort of question that's likely to get a friendly reply but could well lead to further trouble.

Questions need to be treated with the same care that you would use in handling sharp knives. You wouldn't pick up a knife, close your eyes, and just wave it around all over the place. That sort of behaviour would probably cause damage to the people around you and, if they value their safety at all, they would soon scatter and start avoiding you.

Physical damage isn't done with questions but the emotional and psychological damage done may never heal, causing untold damage to a relationship.

However, I don't want to dwell on harmful questions, I want to talk about questions that tend to lift a child's self-esteem, or at least doesn't damage it. This will mean looking at commonly asked questions and suggesting other ways of putting them but I don't want you to dwell on feeling guilty for sometimes putting things in harmful ways, we all do. It's a great achievement if we come to recognize when we have put a question badly because it means we know how to improve the way we put questions in future. All we can expect of ourselves is that we try.

We all know how the emphasis on a word in a question can give it an entirely different meaning. Let's do it to the simple question 'Why did you do that?'.

■ '*Why* did you do that?'
■ 'Why *did* you do that?'
■ 'Why did *you* do that?'
■ 'Why did you *do* that?'
■ 'Why did you do *that*?'

Each question has exactly the same words but each time the meaning of the question is different, depending on the mood of the person asking. One possible meaning to each question would be:

■ The emphasis on 'why' is demanding that the child give a reason for doing it and will probably result in the child having to think up something, fast.
■ The emphasis on 'did' could be asking for a more truthful answer than is usually given and, therefore, implies that the child can't be trusted.
■ The emphasis on 'you' is saying that it was not the behaviour expected from the child and could imply that you think the child is usually above that sort of behaviour.

"ERR, MATTHEW...DO YOU MIND IF I ASK YOU A QUICK QUESTION?"

▨ The emphasis on 'do' could be implying that it wasn't necessary for that to be done at all.

▨ The emphasis on 'that' is saying that there were other things that could have been done.

The simple daily act of asking questions is complicated and can have effects that you don't want to have.

Questions that stimulate development

To stimulate the development of an adolescent by questions means to ask questions that influences them to think about alternative ways of looking at things, or alternative ways of doing things. It means to make them aware that other people look at things differently to them and allow them to compare their way with the ways of other people. In other words, take advantage of the adolescent's tendency to experiment, but ask him questions that will steer him into at least considering the things you want him to think about.

If the child gives an answer there may be a good opening for a talk. But usually your viewpoint is well known to the child and doesn't need any more than a bare mention, unless the child asks questions about it. Just give the information asked for without a long lecture, and let her go off and think about it. Later, maybe even a week or a month later, she may suddenly ask you something else about it and this indicates that she has been thinking about what you said.

Teenagers are in a stage of high intelligence. They are deep thinkers who will take in a small bit of information and think it out but if lectured on a point they will turn off, or think up arguments against the point. I read somewhere that a wise saying should not be explained but left for the person to find their own meaning because any attempt at explanation takes away some of the power of the saying. That also applies to wise questions – they don't always require an immediate answer. Let them think about it and they will get more out of it.

Questions: showing interest or intruding?

Kids will 'clam up' or become defensive if they don't like the questions you ask. Most people seem to dislike a lot of questions being fired at them and yet we expect kids to see our constant questioning as 'showing an interest in what they're doing'. When it comes to the interest being shown through some of the ways we ask questions, kids would probably prefer that we lost interest.

For example, adults wonder why a child answers, 'Nuttin' when they are asked, 'What did you learn at school today?' Parents come to wonder why they bother sending their kids to school at all if they learn nothing and do nothing all day every day.

One likely explanation is that the last thing the child wants to talk about as soon as she gets home is school. This is particularly true of teenagers, who may see school as more of a place for socialising than for learning. Questions about school for these young people need to be carefully worded to separate the work side of school from the social life of school.

For most kids, something like, 'How was your day?' is probably enough because it gives the child the options of a long or short answer as she gets on with the important things, like raiding the fridge.

If you only take one thing from this talk about questions, I would want that thing to be that you avoid using the word 'why' when asking questions of anyone. 'How come?' is only another way of asking why and should also be avoided.

Asking for an explanation for doing something can be very threatening. Usually we don't think about what we are going to do, we know what we want and we just do it. 'Why' means we have to think up a good reason for doing it and we usually think up something that we think the person asking the question will accept.

Instead of asking why, ask the child to tell you what the purpose of the behaviour was:

▧ 'What did you want when you did that?'
▧ 'How did you want that to turn out?'
▧ 'What was the purpose for doing that?'
▧ 'What did you want to gain from doing it that way?'

Asking why is asking them to tell you their inner motive, an elusive thing, but asking for the purpose is much easier to answer because the aim or goal is usually more concrete. However, a child is not likely to want to tell you the purpose of the behaviour if she thinks she will be ridiculed by being told, 'You must be stupid to expect that to happen'.

Another important question is the simple, 'What did you learn from that for next time?' We are so used to asking, 'Why?' that even if we try hard to avoid it we will still use it too often.

Statements

Questions can cause many problems but there is a way that pressure can be put on kids to give information without actually asking them a question. Statements can be used instead of questions when children resent questions or when you want to get a message across to a child and the child refuses to talk.

Statements can also be used to stimulate a person's development by encouraging them to think about their behaviour and its effect on other people, about the different viewpoints held by people, and about different moral values.

Any question can be re-arranged to become a statement. Even the question, 'What's the time?' can be re-arranged to be a statement that calls for information. It then becomes, 'I need to know the time'.

Changing questions into statements puts pressure on people to volunteer information because it appeals to the strong need to belong. People want to help each other and to feel important; giving information helps them feel that they have contributed something. Giving information to someone who needs it is easier and more satisfying than giving it to someone who asks for it, or demands it.

'Why did you do that?' can be changed to an 'I' statement like, 'I can't see the purpose for that way of doing it'.

'Can you explain that a bit better?' can be changed to, 'I don't understand what you mean'.

'Where are you going?' can be changed to, 'I'd appreciate knowing where you intend going tonight' or, 'I need to know where you're going'.

'Can we talk about it?' can be changed to, 'I want to talk about it'.

'Are you on drugs?' can be changed to, 'I am afraid that you might get hooked on drugs'.

Maybe you have asked a couple of questions and got nowhere but you want to get a message across. It's time to use a statement. Simply say something like, 'I don't believe that dope smoking should be legalised but I'm willing to listen to other people's views', and then leave it at that. The problem with this statement is that it has two parts, either of which may bring a comment; whether dope smoking should be legalised or whether you do listen to the views of other people. If you get a comment on either of these, you would be wise to listen to it or 'I'm willing to listen to other people's views' is shown to be untrue.

Another time a statement is useful is when you want to show a child how to do something and the child doesn't want to talk about it. Simply say how you do it and let it go at that.

As mentioned before with regard to questions, just throw in a statement and leave it for the super-intelligent brain of the adolescent to toss around. She might come up with questions about it that will challenge your way of doing it and if you are as willing to listen and learn as you expect her to be, you might learn something yourself.

Sometimes a child will ask a question in a sneering way that is only a cover-up for wanting to know but not wanting to appear to be interested. Just answer the question and don't get hooked into the side issue of the way the question was asked. The important thing is that you give them something to think about and don't take their attention off your answer by mentioning the way the question was put.

Do you argue or discuss?

Getting sidetracked by the way a question is put can lead to arguments and I believe that serious arguments are more likely to retard a child's development than encourage it. It is important to talk with young people and to discuss whatever they want to discuss but I believe that arguing with a young person is harmful to them, and to you, for two main reasons.

Firstly, the more she argues for her present behaviour, the more she is cementing herself into that position and if she stays in that position for long the cement will harden, she will be set in those ways and find it extremely difficult to change. A child who argues long and hard about why she should keep acting the way she does puts pressure on herself to stay that way.

Discussion is different to arguing. Discussion is comparing different ways and different outlooks, without being set into any one set of ideas. Discussion allows your child, or you, to walk out of the cement before it has a chance to set hard.

Trying to understand the other person's point of view in a talk and being willing to alter your own point of view is a discussion. You are arguing when you are determined to keep your own point of view as you try to get the other person to adopt your point of view. Arguments can seriously delay or destroy development. Honest discussion encourages both child and adult development.

The second problem with arguments is that no-one really wins: it is a negative outcome for both. The so called winner may feel a sense of victory but the relationship suffers by the resentment felt by the loser. Is it worth winning if damage is done to the relationship with your child? Serious arguments can harm or destroy relationships. Honest discussion repairs or strengthens relationships.

If you have a set opinion about something and have no intention of changing that opinion, use statements to say what you see as the benefits of it and then let the kid see that it does work for you, by the way you put it into practice.

The emphasis changes a statement

No matter whether they are questions or statements, the emphasis on a word can change the whole meaning of the message. For example, let's look at a simple statement and its different meanings:

- ■ '*I* love you.'
- ■ 'I *love* you.'
- ■ 'I love *you*.'

The first statement says, 'Aren't you the lucky one, that someone as wonderful as me could love you'.

The second statement says, 'I don't hate you or just like you, I have a much deeper feeling for you than that'. The third statement says, 'Of all the people in this world, its you that I love'.

Try this out using various statements and you will soon see that the whole meaning of a statement can be changed by simply putting the emphasis on a different word. Could it be that when your child gets rebellious, she might be hearing the emphasis on a word that makes your statement sound like an order?

Things to think about

✔ Parents, as well as children, have rights.

✔ In problem solving, answering the questions 'who owns the problem initially', 'do I want to help' and 'do I want to accept ownership' are the first steps in the discussion process.

✔ When a child approaches you with a problem, *how* you respond is more important for boosting the child's self-esteem than *what* you decide to do about the problem.

✔ Changing questions into 'I' statements can be beneficial to both the parent and the child.

✔ The emphasis you use in questions and statements can change the meaning of the message.

CHAPTER 8

Who is Responsible for What?

Theories are wonderful but . . .

ONE NIGHT at a parent support group meeting, the guest speaker was trying to make the point that children will act responsibly when they are given the opportunity to take responsibility for themselves. He was interrupted by a mother of six children who said what he was saying was fine in theory but when you have two kids fighting, another playing Tarzan on the clothes line at the same time as another is yelling for a feed, and the other two are packing to leave home, these sorts of theories don't work. Before the speaker had time to answer, another woman agreed with the first and added how much harder it is for mothers than for fathers because he is away all day having peace and doesn't have to worry about how the kids got on at school, or all the other daily parenting problems.

This highlighted the many confusing problems faced by parents who seek knowledge about parenting and try to apply that knowledge in their day-to-day parenting problems.

Who is responsible for controlling the behaviour of the children?

The point the speaker was trying to make was that holding the children responsible for their own behaviour takes all or most of the strain away from the parent, and the child is more likely to take responsibility because he feels more respected.

What sparked that piece of wisdom in the first place was a question from a father about getting kids to do their homework. He talked about the constant battle involved and the amount of time it took to help his children do their homework. The speaker replied that his personal attitude was to help the kids if they wanted help but he would not wreck his relationship with the kids by battling over homework. If they didn't do it they had to face the consequences from the school.

Someone at the back called out, 'But wouldn't the school want you to do something about the problem?' 'Yes', said the speaker, 'But I would tell the school that the problem is between the child and the school. I encourage and support homework but because it is a requirement of the school, and the responsibility of the child to meet that requirement, it is up to them to deal with that problem'.

Again the woman with the six kids gave examples of her problems. She could not see how letting the kids take responsibility for themselves could possibly work in the chaos of parenting six demanding kids (seven, if you count her husband).

There is no way that the problems of that mother could be sorted out in a few short answers but over the next few chapters we will be discussing responsible behaviour, how to hold the kids responsible for their own behaviour, and at the same time give them confidence in themselves. However, at no time will I be saying that it is easy to do.

Back in the days when social workers made the decision as to when and where 'uncontrollable' teenagers could live, we had many incidents of kids in our residential unit acting out. Because they had to stay for a set time or to meet certain conditions, they believed we had to put up with whatever they wanted to dish out to us. The misbehaviour of our uncontrollable kids dropped dramatically when we made their stay with us voluntary, gave them more control and started holding them responsible for their behaviour.

Defining responsible behaviour

Parents are always interested in knowing what to do about irresponsible behaviour but before we can do that properly, we have to know what responsible behaviour is. Whenever I ask people to describe responsible behaviour, they have a fairly clear idea what they mean and yet there are many different definitions given.

> 'It's when people know what they are doing and take the consequences.'
> 'It's behaviour that doesn't do anybody any harm.'

'It's admitting that you did the wrong thing.'

'It's accepting that it is up to you to do something.'

'It means looking after yourself and not expecting others to do things for you.'

'It means paying your debts and being considerate of other people.'

'It means being held accountable for something and if anything happens to it, look out.'

'It means being trustworthy, that you will do what you say you will do.'

Responsible behaviour is all of the above and more. The word 'responsible' is used in many different ways and has many different meanings. The meaning I want to put forward is:

> **⁶Being able and willing to assertively respond to a problem that I have accepted as my problem.⁹**

This is looking at daily life as being a series of little problems that have come about from nature, from the behaviour of other people or as a result of my own behaviour and each problem has to be attended to by someone, spontaneously or by agreement.

Example

There has been a rule made that the cat is to be put out at night and I agreed to accept 'putting the cat out' as my problem. How I respond to that problem decides how 'responsible' I am. If in putting the cat out I cause any harm to the cat or disruption to other people, I have created another problem and therefore a further test of how responsible I am by how I respond to the problem I created. I might deny that I caused the harm or I might hide the damage or I might blame the cat and try to avoid being the one to have to put things right again.

Although I am suggesting that daily life is a series of problems to be solved I don't mean that we have to be making conscious decisions about each of those problems. Most daily life is habit or guided by rules of behaviour that we have learned and agreed with to the extent that we don't see them as rules but as being 'just the way things are done'.

Just to balance things up, daily life is also a series of satisfactions and hopefully the satisfactions outnumber the problems. They no doubt will if your problems are solved to your satisfaction.

We are doing something all day and yet we make very few conscious decisions about how to act. This means there has to be a difference between responsible decision making and responsible behaviour so I will just quickly describe responsible decision making. The reason for separating the two is that it is possible to be good at responsible decision making without being responsible in behaviour.

Responsible decision making

Splitting responsible decision making into *thinking, doing* and *consequences* may help this explanation and alert the parent to what area of responsible decision making needs attention.

Thinking

Before any decision making can take place the child has to become aware of the problem, so discovery is the first element of the 'thinking' part of responsible decision making. The next thinking activity is to think about how to solve the problem and some children need help in thinking up different ways of solving a problem. The child may only know one way and believes it's the only way to handle that problem. Once aware of this, the parent can encourage her to ask her friends or to watch them and others to see how they handle that problem, then discuss the likely outcome (consequences) of those ways.

Observation may reveal that the child knows he has a choice but he has great trouble in making a decision. This is an opportunity for the parent to give him practice at decision making. Start off by often giving him choices between two things like, 'What shirt do you want to wear, the blue one or the green one?' 'Do you want to walk or ride?' 'Are you going to do your homework before tea or after?'

Whatever choice the child makes has to be respected as OK because the important thing is that the child makes a choice. It doesn't matter which one is chosen and it doesn't matter if the parent would have chosen the other one. The child has to feel you respect his choice so he gains confidence in making decisions. Later on, the number of alternatives can be increased to three or even more.

Children who don't learn how to make choices may go on to become adults who agonise every time they are faced with making a choice and desperately try to avoid making decisions. Life can be very difficult for people who need others to make all their decisions for them. I have worked with many young people who want to be locked up in institutions because that is where they feel safe. They don't have to decide anything for themselves and others can control them. As soon as they get out, they do something to get back in.

Doing

Put simply, the 'doing' part of responsible decision making is the following through and doing what was decided or what was agreed on.

Some children will follow through because they accept ownership of the problem. Others will do it because they can't avoid it, others because they will get found out. So the doing part can be a test of whether the agreement was genuine. However, adolescents live for the here and now, so it is normal for them to make agreements and then walk out and forget them, or ignore them, in order to do what is immediately important. As I have said before, normal but not acceptable.

Keeping to agreements is an important part of responsible behaviour but the saying 'Rules are made to be broken' is often used as some sort of justification for not following through with agreements. When rules are made for the safety and fair go of everyone involved, they are not made to be broken.

Consequences

Responsible decision making means being aware of the connection between the behaviour and the outcome or result of that behaviour. A child may be aware that the consequence was the result of the way it was done but simply

"HOME-WORK BEFORE OR AFTER DINNER ? "
" DURING — IT'S HOME ECONOMICS ..... "

being aware of that doesn't mean he will accept that he should do anything about it. He may agree that his behaviour caused a problem but flatly deny that he should put it right.

Using the cat example above, the agreement was that the cat was to be put out and the cat was put out. The rough way the cat was put out may have caused harm to the cat but that was not part of the agreement. More than likely the cat will be blamed for not going out without getting hurt.

If this sort of thing happens maybe the child should only be involved in doing jobs that don't directly involve people or animals. Putting the rubbish bin out may be more appropriate because any carelessness can be more easily dealt with.

According to all the above, as long as a person discovers he has a problem, thinks up alternative ways of solving the problem, chooses an alternative, follows through with the choice and knows the consequences of that decision, it is classed as responsible decision making.

The difference between responsible decision making and responsible behaviour is that the chosen alternative may be very harmful to other people and still show that the child is capable of following proper decision making procedures.

Everyday responsible behaviour

Responsible behaviour is about ownership of problems and assertiveness. The meaning I have given to the word responsible means that ownership of a problem is the most important part of being responsible. Being able and willing to respond or to be assertive are important but nowhere near as important as accepting ownership of the problem.

Assertiveness plays a major role in responsible behaviour because in our day-to-day living, the needs and wants of other people must be respected if we want to be responsible people. Behaviour that puts people at risk or doesn't give them a fair go is unacceptable.

The example of 'putting the cat out' showed that ownership doesn't only mean ownership of the original problem but also ownership of the results of the way the problem was solved.

Observing your child may reveal that he has great trouble owning the consequences when things don't go well. He probably doesn't have any trouble facing up to good consequences, only the bad kind. To learn to own consequences, he may need to have things arranged so he can't avoid facing up to some things and learns that the world doesn't end because of that. Co-operation is the tool to use in teaching a child that he can survive taking consequences. Through this he learns that by making another choice he can alter the outcome to something he is happy to face up to.

'You can't help bad luck', or 'Shit happens' are two sayings kids use to deny ownership of the result of their behaviour as if it was some kind of accident that was beyond their control. I have heard many adults using these same sayings for the same reason. 'It was an accident' seems to work for all ages as an excuse to cover up careless behaviour.

Kids follow the example of adults, and kids will only learn to take responsibility for their own behaviour if adults stop passing off so many acts of carelessness and negligence as accidents.

A speaker from the legal services once told us if we were ever pulled up by the police for speeding we would get off much lighter if we made sure it went to a jury trial by deliberately running over the cop and claiming it as an accident. He put this down to members of juries being nearly all car drivers who don't want to be held responsible for their driving. If what he says is

anywhere near true, adults have a long way to go to become responsible people and it's no wonder kids claim so much of their behaviour as an accident.

There are so few true accidents that it is safe to take the attitude that 'accidents don't happen, they are caused'. Going into the events leading up to a so called accident will reveal a point where a little more care could have been taken.

A kid knocks a cup off the table and says, 'Sorry Mum, it was an accident'. The child doesn't mention that he wasn't looking where his hand was going because this would not be consistent with calling it an accident. He probably didn't deliberately knock the cup, and therefore didn't intend to break the cup, but the circumstances were not beyond his control. The main point I want to make about the breaking of the cup and about accidents in general, is that circumstances are not beyond the control of at least one person who has been involved in the lead up to the incident.

I don't accept accidents. To me, the word 'accident' is an objectionable word that gives some people a feeling of confidence in acting very carelessly.

They don't have to be careful because they can claim bad consequences as being the result of an accident. If the suggestion is made that they accept ownership for things that are popularly called accidents, these people may become quite panic-stricken.

On the other hand, my experience is that most kids, and adults, will become far more careful when they know that the 'accident' excuse will not be accepted and they have to face up to the results of what they do.

Connection between behaviour and consequence

Problems and satisfactions are the consequences of behaviour and it is through learning to control consequences that a child learns to have control of life. Therefore, holding your child responsible for his own behaviour and allowing him to experience the consequences of that behaviour is giving him control of his life.

For a child to learn to behave in a responsible way, that child has to learn the connection between behaviour and the normal consequence of that behaviour. Artificial consequences (punishments) destroy the chances of making the connection between his actions and the consequences of those actions.

There has to be a limit to the range of alternatives a child is allowed to choose from but just because an option is unacceptable to us doesn't mean it's not an option. If parents refuse to acknowledge the existence of unacceptable options they miss out on the opportunity to talk to the kids about those options.

For instance, I would never encourage a child to steal to get what he wants but if I acknowledge that stealing is an option open to him, I can talk about the effects (consequences) of that action for him and for other people. On the other hand, if I just dismiss it as not being an option I miss that opportunity.

The same line can be taken with very controversial things like abortion. If you are against abortion and refuse to consider it as an option, you miss the opportunity to talk about the factual effects on all involved. I'm against stealing and I'm against abortion but, whether I'm talking about stealing or abortion or whatever, there are always some advantages that have to be considered if my opinion is to have any credibility with children. I have to face the inescapable truth that no matter what I think or want, the final decision to steal or get an abortion has to be made by the person faced with that choice, she is the one who will have to live with the consequences, in one way or another.

The abortion example shows the dilemma involved when children start doing things before they are really old enough. Although a young person may be physically mature enough to become pregnant she may not be psychologically or emotionally mature enough to own the delayed or long term consequences of making decisions about things like sexual intercourse or abortion.

The dilemma for those who care about her is that once she has made the first decision and become pregnant as a result (assuming that it was her choice), she has put herself in the position of having to make another decision she is not mature enough to make, and yet no-one else can make it for her.

Young people in this type of situation need all the support and encouragement they can get. The last thing they need is criticism and judgement.

If she feels you have pressured her into doing something she didn't want to do both of you will suffer from her resentment, so she has to be the one to decide. But she has to live with whatever her choice is. Prevention is best, so give her knowledge and support before she has to handle the first choice she faced about sexual activity.

Discipline and control

There is very little difference in the definition of these two words because the word discipline means 'keeping within certain boundaries' and the word control means 'keeping within certain boundaries'.

Initially the parents own the problem of the discipline, or control, of the children but the job of the parents is to gradually get the kids to accept ownership so they have self-discipline, or self-control. There should be a movement from the discipline of the child by the parent to the self-discipline of the child and this handover of ownership of problems commences from the very first thing the child becomes capable of doing for herself.

Once a child has the ability to tie a shoelace, why does the parent tie it for him? Once a child knows that a double knot doesn't come undone and can tie a double knot, it's up to the child if he continues to have his shoelaces come undone. The parent's job is to teach the kids to do things and give them practice at doing them.

Kids who want to have self-control long before they can handle the problems they want to tackle are not displaying the kind of self-control that I see as real self-control. The word 'responsible' is missing and along with it the word 'assertive', with all that word's meaning of considering the needs of others.

Are kids sometimes 'forced' to be irresponsible?

Babies don't have the power or the ability to solve their own problems so they soon learn how to attract those who do have the power (parents) to come and attend to the baby's needs. As we saw earlier, babies learn many things and here we will consider two of them. The first is the lesson that if he were to just lie quietly, he would miss out on a lot of attention and go hungry at times. Secondly he learns the lesson that his happiness depends on other people and his control of them. Naturally he soon develops a strong desire to control other people.

What is true for a baby is true for an adolescent; as long as he behaves himself, he probably won't be noticed. The whole world seems to run the same way, people have to do something out of the ordinary to be noticed. Newspaper reporters only write stories about people whose behaviour has been unusually positive or unusually negative, like the winning of a big sporting event or the robbing of a bank.

The lesson learned by the baby, that happiness and comfort depends entirely on the ability to control the parent, has to be gradually corrected or he may never accept responsibility for his own happiness and will continue to believe it is everybody else's responsibility to keep him happy.

The good news for parents is that it's never too late to be doing something to correct this belief. How? You can make a good start by choosing how you react to what the kids do instead of just doing the first thing you feel like doing. The first thing you feel like doing is probably exactly what they want you to do.

Give choices so he will come to realise that he has a choice in how he reacts to what happens in life and it is through that choice that he has control over his own life, including how he feels.

Think back on your own childhood. Think about the things you used to do to get your own way when you were a child. What sort of things worked for you?

Well-behaved children have problems too

One of the reasons a child becomes confused about what is responsible is because so many people have the attitude that a kid who sticks to the rules is a 'good kid'. But what if a good kid is unhappy about something and no-one is taking any notice of him? What if he doesn't have the ability to speak up for himself? What if he has the ability but isn't lucky enough to have people who stop and listen?

Something very good or very bad has to be done to be noticed but doing something very good may just get a pat on the back and being told to 'keep up the good work, son'. To be really noticed his behaviour has to become a problem to someone, usually the parent, so he falls back on tried and proven ways to get others to take notice. What has worked in the past will work again.

This means he has to make a noise, or break something, or look helpless, or throw a tantrum. Babies, children, adolescents, young adults, parents, and old people all do these things but do them in different ways. Some of those ways are socially acceptable and some are not.

Sometimes teenagers are not able to solve their own problems. Sometimes they don't want to solve their own problems. Sometimes teenagers will want to solve a problem but haven't got the power to solve it. Sometimes a teenager will want the parent to help them solve a problem but their desire for independence will prevent them from asking for help. One thing is certain, there will be times when an adolescent will want to bring attention to the fact that he has a problem.

Separate 'the approach' from 'the problem'

I see no reason why you can't treat this as the child's 'approach' about a problem. It doesn't have to be seen only as an irresponsible approach but can be the only way the child knows to bring attention to his problem. Let me use an extreme example. A 12-year-old child kicking his chair and banging his spoon on the table to attract his mother's attention is a responsible way for a spastic child to act.

The two things need to be separated, the problem the child wants to bring attention to and the method the child uses to get that attention. The spastic child's method is determined by his physical abilities and another child's method is determined by his social skills or his self-confidence level.

There are any number of reasons for a child acting out to bring attention to a problem. Have you ever had a toothache or an earache or headache? A physical pain can affect a child's every action as the pain becomes the centre of his attention and he doesn't feel like considering the needs of other people or listening to their problems. We can understand that type of pain because most of us have been in that position.

Pain is a very personal thing that can't be seen except through the behaviour of the person in pain. Emotional pain is even more personal and although the person in pain may not want to reveal the pain, it dominates the mind and feelings of the person and affects the behaviour.

Many kids 'misbehave' as a result of deep emotional pain that they cannot approach anyone about. This pain may come from sexual or other abuse, from the loss of friends when moving to another town, from the loss of a girlfriend/boyfriend, from the divorce of the parents or from anything that is emotionally important to the child.

Knowing a person has a headache helps us to be tolerant of their behaviour because it usually doesn't last very long but if it went on for a long time something would need to be done before that behaviour became a normal way of acting. Emotional pain can go on for years and so can the bad behaviour.

The behaviour and the pain have to be dealt with separately because they are separate things. Obviously the thing to do is remove the cause of the pain and the behaviour will be different but all the parent can deal with is the behaviour because the child will not reveal the pain. But even when the parent is aware of the pain, the bad behaviour can only be tolerated for so long before it must be dealt with as an inappropriate way of expressing that pain.

Inappropriate behaviour is usually controllable because a person acting badly from a physical or emotional pain is likely to act very differently when someone they want to impress comes into the room. They will put effort into being bright and friendly.

The negative and positive spirals

'Prevention is the best cure' is certainly true when it comes to negative spirals. It is much easier to prevent a child going into a negative spiral than it is to get him out once he gets into it. Preventing it can be done by giving encouragement for effort, for trying, for having a go. Even a simple, 'Good try, well done' can give tremendous encouragement to someone who has missed out on winning.

Most of us are aware of sayings like:

'You cannot give without receiving.'
'The more you give, the more you get.'
'Karma'
'You reap what you sow.'
'You get what you deserve.'

A child is irresponsible in trying to get what he wants and is told, 'You're disgusting'. He then feels bad about himself and a bit dark on the whole world. This bad feeling about himself then leads him to more irresponsible behaviour that confirms his belief about himself and the world and leads to even more negative behaviour.

This sets up the downward spiral that parents refer to when they say , 'I kept trying to get him to behave but he just got worse and worse'.

I want to make it clear that, except when power is being abused, parents are never to blame for the behaviour of a child and the child must be held responsible for his own behaviour. However, the parent is responsible for any action of theirs that keeps the child feeling bad, or for how much effort is made to bring him out of the spiral. This is an important point: the parent may be responsible for a child staying in a downward spiral if the parent makes no effort to bring him out of it, but the child's actual behaviour is his choice, he could have chosen another way.

On the other hand, although a child may not be to blame for being in a downward spiral in the first place, if he is genuinely given the ability and the opportunity to come out of it but decides to continue with his negative behaviour, he becomes responsible for being in that downward spiral and may be on the road to having a personality disorder that will only change by him making a conscious decision to change.

A child who has *chosen* to remain in a negative spiral can be influenced to come out of it by not allowing him to get what he is trying to get by irresponsible behaviour.

We all do irresponsible things at times and it doesn't become a life time thing. These are one-off irresponsible acts. I am talking about the scene where a child does something wrong, gets punished and does more wrong, gets punished some more and so on until the situation deteriorates into an all out riot, out of proportion to the first 'offence' of the child. When these incidents carry over from one day to the next, the child may drop into a negative spiral that traps him for life. It may seem amusing the first time a child says, 'I can't do anything right, I'm rotten, the whole world stinks' but not so funny if it is the start of a negative spiral.

The opposite is also true, that when a child believes he has acted responsibly he thinks well of himself and the world he lives in. He is more likely to repeat the behaviour that resulted in his good feelings and so confirms what he thinks about himself and the world. He may get into a positive spiral that leads to great achievement or to just an 'ordinary' life, which is success enough these days.

Power struggles as part of negative spirals

Power struggles are negative spirals for the parent and the child and this is what makes it so hard to come out of power struggles. Once we get into a power contest with a teenager, it seems unreasonable to expect us to even try to find good things to respond to or acknowledge about this kid who is being so insolent and defiant.

This is why the best weapon to use in a power struggle is to back off. Backing off wins a power struggle because it gives you control and that is exactly what you wanted when you entered the situation. The only difference is that your control is over the situation, not the child. Backing off puts the brake on the spiral and gives you space to be able to look again at the situation to see how you can help the child to come out too.

Moving a child from a negative to a positive spiral

The negative spiral comes from irresponsible behaviour and the positive spiral comes from responsible behaviour. Therefore, if we want our children to get into the positive spiral we have to bring their attention to the responsible things that they are doing and not be constantly keeping their attention on the negative or irresponsible behaviour. After all, the majority of their behaviour is actually positive but because it's just ordinary everyday behaviour we tend to take it for granted and fail to acknowledge it.

Adults complain that kids take them for granted. The kids are entitled to make the same complaint, they may act responsibly all day every day for weeks without drawing a comment but the first irresponsible action brings plenty of notice. Therefore things haven't changed since babyhood: if you want any notice taken around this joint, make a noise.

Education is one of the most powerful ways to move a child from the negative spiral to the positive spiral. I don't mean school education, although that's extremely important, I mean passing on knowledge about anything. If kids know a better way to get what they want, they will usually switch to that way.

Responsible behaviour needs the ability, the opportunity and the desire

Everyone needs three things to act responsibly. They need the *ability*, the *opportunity* and the *desire*. You can give them the ability by teaching them a responsible way of doing it; you can give them the opportunity by accepting their variation of what you teach them, but the desire will only be there if it is accepted by them as a better way, or if they see your example in doing it that way.

The most common method used to try to move a child from a negative spiral to a positive spiral is punishment. But punishment is a form of revenge and revenge is another cycle that becomes a spiral if stretched out over time.

Examples of responsible/irresponsible behaviour

Example 1

A young person may be well aware that the consequence of going out without permission is that he is going to get a roasting from Mum the next day. He gets invited to a party and decides that it's worth going through one of Mum's tantrums to go to the party, so he tells her he's going to the party, that he will be out all night and will be careful of what he drinks. The next day he wanders back home and makes no attempt to hide anything of what happened and makes no attempt to avoid his mother's disapproving words.

The type of party was unacceptable and the child was not allowed to go but were his actions responsible or irresponsible? Depends on your outlook but this kid thought it out, made a decision, carried it out and accepted the consequences. He also let his mother know when to expect him home and assertively accepted ownership of the results of his behaviour.

Example 2

> A young person tells her Mum she will be at a friend's place for the night but has already made arrangements to go to a wild party. She knows her Mum might find out she isn't at the girlfriend's home but decides she will deal with that later. The next day her Mum asks her about her whereabouts the night before and the girl tries to make out her mother must have been confused about which girlfriend she said she was going to stay with. She gets angry and accuses her mother of not trusting her and of always suspecting the worst. When confronted with proof of where she was, the girl admits it and agrees to a consequence of being grounded for a week but breaks the grounding after the second night.

This young person has thought it out, made a decision and carried out that decision but there is a desperate attempt to avoid the consequences by lies and deception. She attempts to put the blame onto her mother, tries to send her on a guilt trip about trust and tries to throw doubt on Mum's understanding of things. Responsible or irresponsible? Was there ownership of the results of her behaviour and assertiveness? I don't think so.

Be hard on the problem but soft on the child

Most of the rest of this book will be about reacting to irresponsible or inappropriate or bad behaviour but I want you to keep in mind that there may be some real deep hurt behind the behaviour. This is why there is a need for the parent to be hard on the behaviour but soft on the child, to be firm about the behaviour being unacceptable but gentle on the child, to reject the behaviour but never reject the child.

Things to think about

✔ Children will behave more responsibly when they are held responsible for their behaviour.

✔ Responsible behaviour can be defined as accepting ownership for a problem and being willing and able to respond assertively to it.

✔ 'Thinking', 'doing' and 'consequences' are handy guidelines to follow for making responsible decisions.

✔ A 'good kid' can have problems too.

✔ Encouraging the children in their positive efforts may prevent attention seeking, irresponsible behaviour.

✔ Reject the behaviour but never reject the child.

CHAPTER 9

Responding to Irresponsible Behaviour

I N THIS CHAPTER we will be talking about the irresponsible behaviour of kids of all ages, not just teenagers, and starting to look at what to do about it. As mentioned before, you probably have more than one child and have to cope with all sorts of behaviour at the same time but here we can only talk about one kind of behaviour at a time.

If you want a general rule to apply when handling irresponsible behaviour, it would go something like this:

> *'Don't allow yourself to be distracted or sidetracked from the behaviour itself and never do what you first feel like doing without giving it some thought.'*

When kids' needs are frustrated they do something about it and it can be useful to group the ways they have learned to get what they want under four headings: power, attention, revenge and inadequacy.

Kids display all of these behaviours at different times and I believe it is wrong to label a child as being any one of these. Saying a child is an attention getter is like saying that she has only one way of reacting to the frustration of not being able to get her own way. All kids want attention and approval but some want more than others. All kids want a feeling of power, to have control, but some want more than others. All kids want revenge when they are hurt but some get hurt easily and may seek revenge more often than others. All kids feel helpless and inadequate at times and need encouragement but some feel this way too often and this can be a real problem.

Self-esteem depends on a feeling of getting enough attention and having enough power, of feeling adequate and being able to keep things even. If kids don't have these things some feel they are almost forced to act in a way that is irresponsible in the eyes of other people, simply because they are not noticed if they behave themselves.

All of the behaviours of a baby or toddler have a purpose and are generally accepted because of the helplessness of the baby in meeting their own needs. If older children are frustrated in getting what they want the same sort of behaviour can occur but now it is classed as irresponsible behaviour because they have a choice in how they act and usually know a responsible way. There are very few kids who don't know how to please people when it suits them.

We can interpret behaviour and relationships from whatever base we choose and it will sound logical. Some look at it from the need for power, some from the need to belong and so on. They are all true because all of us have these needs but relationships are too complicated for any one label to describe them. Therefore, what I am describing are behaviours people use in their relationships, not the people.

Just as each child is likely to use a mixture of behaviours to get what they want, parents will have to use a mixture of discipline styles to handle those behaviours. Regardless of the age of the child you will sometimes have to intervene by being firm and directive, sometimes be interactive and sometimes be non-directive.

Power struggles

Knowing you are in a power struggle

Power struggles are the main relationship problem between parents and teenage children, as the kids are trying to get more freedom than the parents are willing to give them. Many parents just give up and do nothing, let their kids do as they like and leave the problem to other people and the police.

These parents swing from being too directive to being too non-directive, probably because of the very nature of power struggles being that there has to be a winner and a loser.

You think you are in a power struggle with a child but how can you know? Firstly, because you are trying to get her to keep to agreements and rules.

Secondly, the most common feeling you get when she acts irresponsibly is frustration that leads to anger. Your anger increases your attempts to get her to do what is supposed to be done but it still doesn't happen. This leads to an explosion and either the child gives in or you do.

Whenever the child has to give in she resents you and whenever you have to give in you feel resentment towards her, so the relationship is going downhill fast. There seems to be no way out because no matter who wins, there is resentment.

Power struggles are about what should or shouldn't be done by someone. The parent is trying to direct the child to do something that the child doesn't want to do or the child is trying to get the parent to do something the parent doesn't want to do.

Whatever 'it' is, isn't being done the way one person wants it done. 'It' can take the form of time limits, an untidy room, what sort of friends, where to go.

Active defiance

Active power struggles are when the child is more or less openly saying, 'You can't make me do anything I don't want to do'. As the parent in this sort of situation, you can feel that you have to win this fight to keep your authority, that if you don't get the child to obey then you have lost your authority.

In fact, the opposite is more likely to be true. For the parent to win the immediate fight may be at the expense of damaging the relationship by prolonging the war.

A power struggle is a win/lose situation. Someone has to lose for someone to win. One has to lose face and feel the resentment that leads to future struggles or maybe to feeling helpless and withdrawing to spend a lot of time alone. Some kids retreat to the bedroom, sometimes even to eat meals.

If the parent is the winner, he probably feels he has disciplined the child but does the child really give in or just move to passive defiance and 'forget' to do it? Does the child give in this time but not bother to ask next time? Does the child withdraw and become more dependent on the parent, move from a power struggle to feelings of helpless inadequacy? Did the parent really win?

As parents, we may want to have control of the child when all we really need is control of our parenting. Trying to control the child will lead to the power struggle but controlling our parenting will lead to the child taking responsibility for herself.

In the first interview with any child referred to me as 'uncontrollable' I made it very clear that none of our staff had any authority over her and could not make her do anything. By doing this I only told the kids what they already knew and had set out to prove. Why should I give them more opportunity to prove it? There are plenty of people they can prove that to; I wanted to talk to them about more important things and didn't want to waste time giving them practice at beating me.

At the same time I said things like, 'I can't make you do anything and I have no authority to tell you what to do unless you give me that authority. But it also works the other way, you can't make me do anything either. There are things I can do for you and there are things you can do for me. I can't make you do things for me and you can't make me do things for you, we are equal in that, so I intend to do what I can for you and I expect you to do things for me.'

However, given that kids soon forget agreements, it wasn't long before a power struggle type situation came up and I felt the same desire to control that parents do. Years of experience at making mistakes has taught me that if I am angry at all, back off but don't back down. This allowed both of us a little time to rethink, it may only have been a few minutes but it is the breaking of the usual sequence that is important.

You could try a simple, 'We'll have to settle this but not while we're angry. Let me know when you're ready to talk about the agreement we made yesterday.' Or what about, 'I don't want to talk about it until I calm down.' Or if you want a couple of minutes to get your thoughts together try this one, 'We'll talk about that after I go to the toilet'.

What you both need is a little time to think and the hidden message to the child is that you value the relationship too much to wreck it by fighting.

Being firm without getting into a power struggle

However, if I have to stand my ground, experience has taught me to use only what I have complete control over. I have complete control over my willingness to co-operate, that is, what I am prepared to do and not prepared to do. I have complete control over my enthusiasm, interest, approval, sympathy, and permission. None of these things can be taken from me because they come from within myself.

I also have complete control over whether I argue or not. Trying to have the last word is just another kind of power struggle and, like all power struggles, the best way is not to get hooked into them in the first place. But once I realise I have been hooked, I just back off and pull out.

To avoid getting into a power struggle, be careful about giving direct orders or using anything that can be taken from you or can be defied. Switching a TV set off can lead to a physical struggle if the child decides to 'have a go'. Taking a book or anything else away from a child can have the same result. Locking a child in a room can lead to a broken window. Refusing to let them have a meal can lead to food 'stolen' from the fridge. All of these things can develop into a power struggle.

Passive defiance

Power struggles are not necessarily from open defiance. The main point made above is that something isn't being done and this doesn't have to happen from open defiance. Some kids will be most agreeable but the job still doesn't get done. She'll agree to clean up her room but doesn't do it. She will have an excuse every time, like 'I forgot'. It can't be said that there was a fight, but the room remains a mess. You get frustrated and angry and try threats and punishments but you still can't get her to do what you want her to do. She is being passively defiant, but defiant just the same.

A child's bedroom can become one of the few things in life the child has control over and the only way she can show this is by the bedroom being different to the rest of the house. How different it is can be an indication of her general feeling of control over life and this is why it becomes a common source of power struggles.

I would like to be able to tell you that putting the responsibility of keeping the room tidy back on to the child will do the trick but it may not. Maybe the room will get cleaned up but if it isn't done to your satisfaction, close the door and don't go in. Then you don't have to know what it's like and if the smell comes out to meet you then bring that up with the child. It's not worth wrecking a relationship over an untidy room.

Maybe instead of setting how clean the room should be, you can get her to agree to set what she sees as the minimum level for a bedroom and this leaves her free to be cleaner if she wants to. I believe it is better to give children the opportunity to do better than expected rather than be always failing to live up to a set high level.

I overheard a former neighbour of mine trying to deal with his passively defiant 3-year-old-son. The child just stood motionless as his frustrated father said:

> *'I'm telling you for the last time, shut the gate. I told you, I'm telling you for the last time, shut the gate! How many times do I have to tell you that I'm telling you for the last time?'*

Then turning to me he said, 'Oh heck, what can you do with a kid like that?'

I don't know why the father was trying to get the kid to close the gate when the father was the one who wanted the gate closed. Over the years, these two continued to have a lot of power struggles and even into adulthood the son won every time, with the father still saying, 'What can you do with a kid like that?' The simple reply is, 'Don't get into the power struggle in the first place'. Once you are in a power struggle, it's difficult to get out of, so why get into it?

Domestic violence

In talking about power struggles, I cannot ignore the tremendous problem of domestic violence but I hope my real contribution towards this problem will be that at least one person will decide to use non-violent parenting as a result of reading this book. Maybe I can give just one person another way of handling problems.

It seems that the old saying, 'power corrupts and absolute power corrupts absolutely' is true. There is a great power imbalance in families. Parents hold far more power than most of them realise but the real problem comes when the parents constantly want that power to be acknowledged by obedience.

There is no doubt in my mind that men are the greatest offenders when it comes to domestic violence and that no excuse can be accepted for that violence. I also believe that the level of male violence depends on their level of power.

However, even women who have been blamed, put down, bashed and otherwise violated for so long that they actually believe they deserve to be treated that way, may use violence trying to control their kids. This seems like a contradiction but is understandable if you consider that the abuse of power and the use of violence is a human problem, not just a male problem.

Men abuse their power over women. Women abuse their power over children and children abuse other children that they have some kind of power over. The saying, 'Children can be cruel' usually refers to children's emotional cruelty to each other but all schools, and many families, have a problem with physical violence between the kids.

Wife bashers and child abusers all have one thing in common besides abusing their power, they never truly accept responsibility for their behaviour. They don't own the results of their behaviour and even when they are expressing remorse, they will attempt to blame someone else, usually the victim.

Anger management courses are usually recommended for people who use violence to solve their problems. I see little sense in that because most violent people can manage their anger quite well, they always wait until they are in a position of power before they bash. A violent man doesn't bash his boss, he waits until he gets home and takes it out on the wife and kids. Those who would benefit from such courses would be those who don't know any other way to handle problems but it would be rare to find people like that.

Unfortunately, violence is an acceptable way to solve problems and is promoted by TV, videos, sport and news media.

The main reason people use violence is to get what they want when it suits them, and some people (men, women and children) have found that violent behaviour will get them what they want most of the time. That sort of behaviour will only change when the use of violence fails to get them what they want.

Revenge

Self-defence, or feeling defensive, happens whenever we feel that we are under attack from the words or actions of others, so whenever we feel defensive it's a sure sign we have either been hurt or are in danger of being hurt, and when someone hurts us we hurt back. There is nothing wrong with self-defence but when our self-defence becomes an attempt to 'get even', it has become revenge.

Two people who are hurting each other set up a cycle of revenge and that cycle can only stop if one of them decides to stop hurting the other.

As the more mature person, it is the parent who should stop first and by doing so take control of the situation. Sometimes taking control can mean apologising in an assertive way such as, 'I became angry when you called me names and I insulted you back. I'm hurt about what you said but I'm sorry I hurt you back'. A sincere apology from an adult to a child is a powerful way of gaining the confidence of the child.

In some relationships it is worth remembering that showing you are hurt is telling people how to succeed at hurting you if that's what they want to do. Once they know what will hurt you, they can use it as revenge and as a means of controlling you. Who do you want to be in control of the situation, you or the other person? Well don't let them get what they want by their behaviour.

Words don't offend, people do

A common cause of revenge is the hurt feeling kids get when they believe they are being talked down to, being treated like 2-year-olds. Of course the fact that they have been acting like two-year-olds most of the day is supposed to be overlooked.

It's very difficult to understand or predict what will hurt or offend people because a person can be offended by a word or gesture in one situation and not be offended by that same word or gesture in another situation. Or a person can be offended by a word or gesture from one person and not from another person.

On many occasions I have spoken to young people on this point, after a fight that was the result of one being offended by insulting words thrown around by the other. During the talk I sometimes use the same words to the one that was offended by them and there is no reaction. In fact at times the child will laugh when I use the same words in the same way as the person whose head he had just tried to pound in. When asked why he didn't hit me he says, 'But that's different, you're not him'.

From this it appears that the words were not as offensive as the mouth they came out of. I see this as an attempt by the child to blame the other kid for his own inability to cope with something else about that kid but this is a concept that is very difficult for an adolescent to see.

If the insulting words came from the parent, then the words were not the problem, it was the fact that those words came from someone the child always looked to for comfort and protection. Now even that person is abusing her.

Hurting a child without knowing it

Maybe the child is hitting out at the parent because she believes they failed to rescue her from a hurtful situation at some time. The parent may not even be aware that the child was ever in the situation but, from the child's point of view, the parent has failed to protect her and it really only matters what the child perceives to be the truth when it comes to understanding the reason for the feeling of hurt that causes the action of revenge. Maybe the child was badly affected by the divorce of the parents and maybe blames the parent she is living with for driving the other parent away.

Parents are usually completely unaware that their child has been sexually abused by a neighbour or family friend but, in the eyes of the child, parents are supposed to protect their children from danger and she was not protected from danger.

Maybe the child believes that she told the mother about the incident and the mother didn't do anything about it. Children can sometimes give cryptic messages that they believe are quite clear and they may do this when the parents are busy and not really listening. The parent can't be blamed for being unaware of the incident and can't really be blamed for not understanding the cryptic message but this doesn't alter the fact that the child believes that the parent has failed to protect her or has done nothing about it. The hurt for the child is no less and it is the hurt that brings about the actions to cause the parent pain, a pain that the parent believes is unjustified but that the child believes is well justified.

Getting into a cycle of revenge with the kids will only make things worse. Don't hit back at them. Be firm but always be aware that they only hurt you when they feel hurt and maybe a hug is the most appropriate response.

Need for attention and approval

Backing off from a power struggle is difficult and so is pulling out of a revenge cycle but nothing is as hard as handling chronic attention getting behaviour.

Kids who are constantly after attention can drive parents to the edge of insanity and the thing that can tip them over is the advice that people give on how the parent should handle the attention getting: 'Just ignore him, he's only after attention'.

Parents feel bound to respond

Real attention demanding kids will do anything to dominate the time of the parent and some of those things the parent cannot ignore. Some of the behaviour is self-destructive, some of it is aimed at hurting other people, animals or property. All of these things the parent has some obligation to protect and the child knows it, that's why he does it. There would be nothing to gain in doing it if the parent didn't feel bound to respond.

The attention demanding child has gained control of the parent. This is something the parent has to admit if there is to be any hope of improving the situation. The evidence of this is that as soon as the parent gets the child to stop one annoying behaviour, she starts doing something else.

Continually annoying the parent in order to get something has probably been a longstanding method used by the child and this has not changed. Why does she do this? Because it has worked in the past to get what she wants and 'when you're on a good thing, stick to it'. Why should a child change a method that works so well? One more question, who makes it work for her?

While it is succeeding to get what is wanted, there will be no change so it is up to you to stop allowing it to work. 'Here we go, a bit more parent bashing', you might be thinking. No, I would like to see the victim stop being a victim and take charge of the situation by being assertive.

Hurting others to gain attention

Real attention getting doesn't care whether the attention gained is yelling, scolding or smacking, it's still attention and this is part of what makes attention getting behaviour so difficult to handle.

You may think you have had a little win by sending the child to her room but as soon as the door is closed she starts banging on the door, or throwing things around, or turning the music up full bore, or yelling out, anything at all to keep your attention. Anything at all so you don't forget she is around. Anything at all to dominate your time.

The domination of your time may be done by hitting the other kids so you will have to intervene. Some kids discover a great attention getting power in threats towards younger children. The parent is not game to leave the kids alone because of a fear that the older child will do some damage to the smaller kids. More than likely he has never done them any real harm and won't do them real harm, but the actions are threatening and the parent is not willing to take the chance. Either the young child or the older one has to be with the parent at all times and this is very demanding on the parent.

Maybe you decide to send the others outside and keep her beside you so she can't hit them and, because she keeps annoying you to let her go outside with the others, you think she has been punished.

Even if you become aware that she has controlled you again and send her outside, there is no doubt that within a very short time something will happen to force you to notice her, by hitting the other kids again or maybe just by peering at you through the window. She has your attention again.

Generally:

> *'If you can't ignore the behaviour, give it as little attention as possible'.*

"IGNORE HER - IT'S JUST ATTENTION - GETTING BEHAVIOUR... "

Being 'super-nice'

The other side of the coin is the child who gets attention by being 'good' to the point of being annoying. This is still attention seeking and can be just as demanding as the 'bad' behaviour, except that other people will be constantly remarking on what a good girl she is. This can lead to Mother feeling guilty for being annoyed with her and wanting her to stop being so nice.

It's very difficult to deal with a person who is being super-polite and nice, doing things for you that you would rather do yourself, wanting to help you in everything you do, interrupting your reading so politely that you feel guilty about the annoyed tone of voice you used to answer her. She talks to you about anything and everything, generally keeping your attention on her and away from the other kids. She is still dominating your time but doing it so nicely.

Involving the school and the police

Coping with the behaviour at home is hard enough but there may be regular calls from the principal about your child's behaviour at school. You are being called up to the school so often people think you work there. She has forgotten to take her lunch or books. 'Come and pick her up because she is sick'. All sorts of reasons for you to be spending a lot of time attending to her at school.

As the child grows into adolescence the form of the behaviour may change but the purpose of the behaviour remains the same; to dominate the parent's time and keep attention on herself. At adolescence the behaviour may become more public than just involving the school. Now the behaviour may become so public that the police become involved and through this she discovers another way of keeping your attention.

When the public is involved:

> *'Deal with the situation but give her as little attention as possible'.*

When you try to fix it things get worse

What are you going to do about it? First of all admit that the child is controlling you. Then ask yourself, 'Do I really want to do something about it or has it become such a normal way of life that I rather enjoy being able to talk to my friends about this kid?' Do you seek help only to be able to say that no-one can suggest anything that works?

I believe there are many parents who actually don't want this situation to change, for whatever reason, and that's fine, it's their choice.

If you have decided that you want to do something about it, there is something else you have to face: when you try to get control of the situation, the behaviour will get much worse and this is why it seems the advice you have been given doesn't work.

It may help to think of the attention getting as turning into a power struggle in which the child is using attention as the weapon. When she thinks she is starting to lose control, the child will throw everything she's got into the struggle to regain control. She may use 'unfair' tactics like breaking things, or hitting smaller kids, or being cruel to the cat, things you can't ignore.

When people and/or property are in danger:

> *'Do what you have to do to protect
> people and property but do it silently or
> use as few words as possible'.*

There is no doubt that ignoring attention getting behaviour is the best way to handle it but there are times when you can't ignore it. The next best thing is to give it as little attention as possible by dealing silently with the behaviour. Say nothing, just do what you have to do to protect someone but do it without a word to the attention seeker, if possible, or by only saying what absolutely has to be said.

When it comes to property, it is very difficult to turn your back on someone who is threatening to break something you value but the long term benefit may outweigh the short term cost.

Do you still want to do something about it? Then be warned, you are going to need a lot of patience.

Your child needs love and attention, he needs to feel he belongs and is important. This is the driving force behind this behaviour at home, at school and in public.

The fact that the attention is manipulated into existence doesn't seem to matter as long as it does exist and the child can feel important and loved. However, the child who demands a lot of attention has few friends.

Now don't go all soft on me because I've said that. The last thing we need now is a sentimental parent. The going will get tough and you'll need to be tough to resist giving in. Try to keep in mind that you are striving for a better future for yourself and your child. If you go soft he and you are in for a miserable life.

You can give him as much love and attention as you like but don't do it at the times that he is looking for it, you pick the time and do it when he is doing something responsible or is just sitting quietly. These are probably the rare times that you see as a break from attending to him but you may have to sacrifice some of that time now to get more of it in the future.

Inadequacy, depression and suicide

Australia currently has an unacceptably high level of youth suicide and it is generally acknowledged that feelings of inadequacy and depression play a big part in suicide. Why am I saying so little about inadequacy and depression? Because this whole book is about helping kids and parents feel adequate through taking control of their lives and being responsible for their own behaviour. It is aimed at preventing that major cause of suicide from existing in the first place, or from continuing, by helping you to help your child manage her problems and gain control of her life.

People who feel they have no control over what happens, or feel they can not cause things to change, feel helpless. Depression and suicide can result from people feeling that they can't do anything to end their pain. This is even more so for young people; they are at a stage of life where they are likely to believe they will always feel the way they feel right now.

So much in the life of our young people seems pointless and irrelevant. Unemployment removes the purpose from school work that to a 13- or 14-year-old is going to stretch out forever, with nothing at the end. Add the normal relationship problems that kids have, along with problems at home where they should be getting encouragement and support, and all the child wants to do is end the pain. They don't want to die, they just want to end the pain.

Kids need encouragement and support to find satisfactions in things other than paid employment, to find achievements in everyday family life and through activities such as sport or in voluntary work. However, there is little hope of doing that in a system that focuses our whole education system on training people for nonexistent jobs and leaves the kids with no hope of getting a fair share of the wealth of this country.

Youth suicide is another thing that some people blame on the discipline style used by the parents. This is absolute nonsense. Parents have no more control over that decision than they have over any other decision made by a child and it is cruel to hang such blame on parents.

I don't intend to dwell on the subject of suicide or to give the confusing list of things that can indicate a kid could be suicidal. What I am going to tell you is that if you are in any way concerned about a possible suicide, seek help. The easiest and quickest way is to ring Lifeline. You can ring Lifeline at any time and be assured of being able to talk to someone who knows what to advise you to do and no-one need know.

Risk taking

Unfortunately, risk taking seems to be part of teenage behaviour but although risk taking may be very dangerous, it doesn't mean the child is suicidal. However, there is cause for alarm if the risk taker is a depressed child who is on drugs, has emotional problems and knows someone who has succeeded in suiciding.

Some kids are so situational that as far as they are concerned they can be acting responsibly when they are responding to the *now* situation. Adults may see it as totally irresponsible because the adults are looking further down the track.

Health will often be put at risk for a short term thrill. Kids are aware of how AIDS and STDs can be avoided and they are aware of the dangers involved in casual sex but these things are too far into the future, it may take years before AIDS becomes apparent and it may never happen anyway. What is here and now is the thrill of the present situation and some kids can't see past that 'right-here-and-now-not-in-fifteen-minutes-time' situation.

For a girl to ask the boy she is 'in love with' to use a condom is just not on. If we are aware that the real purpose of the girl's behaviour is to appear to be swept up in the moment and not be a girl who normally has casual sex, then it becomes understandable that she doesn't carry a condom or ask that one be worn. I'm not saying it makes it any more responsible, just more understandable.

Young people have sex when they have a meaningful relationship with someone, when they are 'in love' with the person. The amazing thing is how quickly some young people form these meaningful relationships and 'fall in love'. Their 'here and now' attitude allows this falling in love to occur and move to fulfilment the first night of the relationship. Even on these occasions, some young people will claim that there was no need for a condom because, 'He wasn't the kind of boy who would have AIDS, I can tell'.

The quicker sex and love can be separated the better. The quicker romantic love can be promoted and seen for what it is, the foreplay for sex, the better.

Kids are confusing their sexual feelings with being 'in love' and are not helped by the adults who go all 'gooey' about young love.

There are many types of risk taking behaviour that ignores the obvious and real dangers. I watched a TV segment once on the number of young people who had been injured and made quadriplegic as a result of diving off a cliff into a pool and even while the crew were filming the area, there were young people diving into the water. A 14-year-old who had been present the day before when another kid was seriously injured was being interviewed. He laughed and said something about, 'Well, that's how it goes, you've got to die from something'. The only thing he was anxious about was that the interviewer was taking up time that he could be using jumping into the water.

That same boy was probably quite good at making short term decisions but it could hardly be said that he was mature enough to be making decisions about his long term future. There would be every likelihood that he would have the same attitude towards sexually transmitted diseases and drunk driving but he could not be classed as suicidal – foolish maybe, but not suicidal.

All the laws and warnings in the world will not stop risk taking in young people. We can only try to make sure they are aware of the consequences and do all we can to discourage it, then hope and pray they survive.

Guilt

Guilt is one of the most powerful ways a child uses to get his own way. Kids will use this weapon in many ways, some quite subtle like, 'Parents are supposed to trust their kids', which is commonly used to stop the parent from checking with the parent of the friend she claims she is going to stay the night with.

The classic one is, 'I didn't ask to be born', which is an attempt to hold the parent responsible, through guilt, for everything the child does. Another common one that I find hard to understand for two reasons is, 'I'll steal the money and if I get caught it'll be your fault'. One, he is the one who chose to steal and two, why will it only be your fault 'if I get caught'?

'Parents are supposed to care about their kids and help them' is another one that is designed to make parents squirm but it usually comes after the parent has said 'no' to something that's harmful to them anyway.

'Yeah, I s'pose you never made a mistake when you were my age'. This works wonders in getting parents to allow all sorts of irresponsible behaviour.

None of these can make you feel guilty unless you let them. Kids use these common sayings to move your attention away from their behaviour so they don't have to face up to what they're doing. Listen closely and see how often the kids (and others) try to move the blame onto you and take the attention off their behaviour. How often do they succeed in controlling you in this way? Later on we will look at ways to keep the attention on their behaviour but, for now, don't do what you first feel like doing; don't allow yourself to become defensive. Becoming defensive is a sure sign that you have been sent on a guilt trip.

Guilt is a feeling every parent is familiar with and many parents feel guilty about the behaviour of their children. Guilt can be good and I hope I will always feel guilty when I do something that is unfair or results in harm because it is the guilt that will get me to do something about the harm. I also hope that once I have made up for what I've done wrong I can forgive myself for doing it, even if the other person refuses to forgive me.

In order to learn from it, I'll try not to forget what I did but I will not feel guilty or allow other people to get me to feel guilty about things that are not under my control or are no longer under my control. The past is one of the things I have no control over. I can make up for past actions when I get the chance but I can't change the past, it happened.

Things to think about

✔ The teenager can engage in a power struggle using passive defiance as well as active defiance.

✔ Domestic violence and child abuse is caused by people who abuse their power and never accept responsibility for their behaviour.

✔ Revenge behaviour results from two people hurting each other – as the more mature person it is up to the parent to stop hurting the teenager.

✔ Teenagers can only send parents on guilt trips if parents let them.

CHAPTER 10

Changing Children's Behaviour

All behaviour has a purpose

THE PURPOSE OF ALL human behaviour is to satisfy a need or want of our own. This is not a put down of people, it is meant in the context of the joy that the giving of a present brings to the person who is giving.

Most of the 'selfish' needs that we satisfy in doing things for other people are hidden from us. We are not aware of them but they are there. I might give because I feel good doing it or the giving may be done to preserve a relationship that I value and want to keep. Either way, I am doing it because I want to, because it satisfies a need I have to preserve that relationship. Even when the parent is slaving to satisfy the wants of the child, the parent may be unaware that she is satisfying her own need to avoid feeling like a failure as a parent, so in that sense her slaving is done to satisfy her own needs.

All of your behaviour has a purpose and so does all the behaviour of your child. It would be fair to say that if you knew the purpose behind your child's behaviour, his behaviour would probably make sense to you. You still may not approve of what he does but it would make sense.

Your child doesn't always know the purpose of your behaviour and no doubt finds it hard to understand what you're doing at times, it just doesn't make sense to him at all. One reason for this is that he doesn't know your problems and can't possibly know your problems like you know them, just as you don't know his problems and can't possibly know his problems like he knows them.

Change

At adolescence, the problems of the child change, their interests change and their way of getting what they want can change, and be changeable. A normally obedient child can become defiant, a nagging child can become withdrawn, a defiant child can become co-operative, a thoughtful child can become hurtful, a hurtful child can become considerate of other people, and they can be 'one with the lot'. The swinging from one way of acting to another can lead the parent to believe that the child has a split personality and needs psychiatric care. It generally just means the child is an adolescent.

When it comes to changing we seem to want the other person to change first. We claim that we are willing to change but it is the other person who is being difficult. We say, 'You scratch my back and I'll scratch your's'. This seems like a fair enough deal but it really is a cop-out because it means I don't have to do anything to fix the relationship until you do something first. But if both of us take the same stand, we both get out of doing anything and can blame each other.

This is a very common problem between parents and teenagers. Many parents say they're willing to improve the relationship but it has to be the child who makes the first move and therefore it is the child's fault that there's no improvement. This is another area where the parent can take control of the situation and lead the way to a better relationship, even if they only change it to, 'Let's scratch each other's back'.

The difference between needs and wants

In this crazy world it's sometimes difficult to work out the difference between what we need and what we want. The commercial world would have us believe that we need whatever they are selling and the general attitude seems to be that we should have everything we want.

When white people first came to this country they didn't discover Australia, they discovered the difference between needs and wants. The Aboriginal way of living was to satisfy human needs and anything above that state is a want, not a need. We have a need for shelter but a modern home is a want. We have a need for food but a 'Big Mac' is a want. We have a need for fun but video games are a want. We have a need to belong but a string of club memberships is a want. We have a need for importance but a string of credit cards is a want. Is a car a need or a want? If you want to live the 'good life' it's a must but you may have noticed that the word 'want' is involved. Do we have to have the best?

If we are confused about which things are needs and which things are wants, and we are the ones giving the example to our kids, is it any wonder that the kids are confused about it?

I'm not trying to say that it's wrong to satisfy wants, we all have wants and we all try to satisfy them. The important thing is that knowing the difference between needs and wants may make it easier to get our priorities sorted out.

What do you want to change about the kids?

'That seems like an easy enough question to answer. I want the kids to behave themselves, I want them to act responsibly and do as they're told for a change. I want them to change their attitude towards me and stop being so stubborn.'

Yes, but what exactly is it about them that you want to change? Do you really want to stop him from being so stubborn? Do you really want to stop her from manipulating?

I used to work in electronics and in that profession there is a saying that 'any true statement can be reversed and still hold true'. It means that you can take a true statement, reverse it and that opposite will also be true. Sounds silly? Let's see how it can be applied to the behaviour of children and other people.

'John's biggest fault is his stubbornness.' The reverse of this would be, 'John's greatest strength is he refuses to give in'.

What about this one, 'Her manipulating of people will prove to be her greatest liability in life.' This would become, 'Her ability to turn situations to her advantage will prove to be her greatest asset in life'.

'The way she constantly asks questions will make her very unpopular one day.' Change this to 'Her curiosity could lead her to fame as a research worker one day'.

When trying to change the faults of a child we should be very careful that we are not trying to extinguish a strength that is causing us a problem at the moment but which would be very valuable to the child in the future. For instance, stubbornness may cause you a problem now but that same stubbornness will get the child through some tough spots in the future when stamina is called for. When things seem hopeless and there is a need for someone to just keep going against all odds, stubbornness is called determination. Later in life the child may be facing hardship that will need him to just hang in there and that is when stubbornness will see him through.

The same applies to a child whose manipulation is causing trouble at the moment. In the future that ability to manipulate will become a strong management skill or organising skill. The manipulator is able to judge a situation and arrange things to get maximum advantage from it for himself. A good manager is able to take advantage of situations and arrange things to get the maximum benefit for the business.

Being curious and asking a lot of questions was probably seen as a fault in many kids who later went on to become famous journalists or research scientists.

Now have another look at what you want to change about your child and try to see how that fault or weakness can be seen as a strength. What you now see as negative can be looked at as a positive, or at the very least can have something positive about it.

Looking at your child now, is it his stubbornness you want to change or is it the things he is stubborn about? Do you want to stop her from manipulating or to guide her so her management skills don't cause others a problem. Does this mean that instead of stopping the behaviour you really should be encouraging it? Encouraging the very fault you wanted to correct?

Look for the positives about the behaviour and maybe that will give you something to encourage instead of condemn. The quick hand of the shoplifter could become the swift hand of the magician if given the chance and the encouragement. The attention seeker may become an entertainer who works hard to keep the attention of his audience. The kid who yells a lot may be an undiscovered opera singer.

Have you decided yet what it is that you want to change? Maybe the next section will help.

Deciding what you can change

You can change nothing.

You can change your whole world.

Again we have two opposites and, as we saw in the previous section, it all depends on your outlook, an outlook that you can change, if you want to. An optimist will look at a bottle and see it as half full and a pessimist will look at

"**WHAT DO YOU MEAN YOU'VE CHANGED YOUR ROOM AROUND?**"
"**WELL ... I'VE HEAPED THE DIRTY CLOTHES IN THE OTHER CORNER**"

the same bottle and see it as half empty. A pessimist might comment on what a cold day it is and an optimist might comment that it isn't as cold as it could be.

First of all, let's look at a couple of things we try to do that are impossible. We constantly wish the past was different and we try to force kids to change.

One of the reasons members of families find it so hard to get along is that they are constantly bringing up things from the past that don't really matter anymore. Things that someone did two years ago, and longer, will be constantly dragged up and fought over and it doesn't get resolved.

There is nothing about the past that we can change, it happened. But it isn't until we come to accept that the past happened, and cannot be changed in any way, that we can move on to enjoy now and look forward to the future.

It's a bit like grieving over a death, it isn't until we come to the stage of acceptance of what has happened, that it is final and nothing will change it, that we can start to adjust our lives and look to the future. I want you to accept that the past is dead and gone, there is only the present and the future left and both of these you can do something about.

However, there may be a lot of resistance from some members of the family because the person who keeps bringing up the past holds a certain never ending power, because there is absolutely nothing that can be done about it. When more than one member of the family is doing this it becomes a form of power struggle, or can be just a game to stop them from facing the real problems in the relationships and prevent any change.

The second thing we can't do is force kids to change. We cannot make anybody do anything and the kids know it. Even if you do offer a big enough bribe or they want to avoid a big enough punishment, you have not changed their beliefs and values. It just meant he decided to take the bribe or avoid the punishment. You didn't make him do it, you just thought you did.

Now let's get back to where we started. You can change nothing if you try to change the world but you can change your whole world if you change yourself. And by changing yourself, you change what other people are reacting to, so they have to react in a different way. Complicated isn't it?

A young girl said to me one day, 'You know, Bob, I've noticed that the mornings when I get up in a happy mood, everybody's in a good mood, but when I get up in a bad mood, everybody starts arguing and fighting'

She had discovered a great truth about people and about relationships. That people will usually react differently when they are treated differently and that it is possible for her to control her own little world. Maybe she had only just made the transition from one stage of adolescent development to the next and was becoming more aware of herself in relation to other people.

None of us can force anyone to change their beliefs, their values, or their behaviour but everyone of us can have a great influence on others, especially children, to change their beliefs, their values, and their behaviour, simply by changing the way we react to them.

We want immediate change

One of the reasons we use violence and threats so much is because we expect to see big differences immediately, this is the age of 'instant' everything and we expect big changes to occur in the kids when we try to get them to change.

The quickest way to get change is to use violence or force but change that occurs through force only remains while the parent is around to use that force. Change that occurs through influence may last for ever and spread through generations. You may not always see the change that comes from your influence but it is there. The people who brought out a few rabbits and foxes early in the history of white settlement of Australia probably didn't live to see the tremendous effect their behaviour would have on Australia's future.

Ideas are like rabbits. They may have a small beginning and appear to take a long time to spread very far but, given a few generations, they can take over a whole country. When we influence the beliefs and values of a child we are influencing many generations to come.

Suggesting change is not laying blame, it is alerting parents to the habit they've dropped into of allowing themselves to be controlled by others, especially the kids. It is also empowering parents to control their world and take charge instead of being directed by whatever happens. You can take control of your life and have a tremendous influence on other people but it means looking at things a little differently. It means changing the way you look at who is responsible for improving relationships. Changing the way you treat other people so they change the way they treat you. To take control so you get treated the way you think you should be treated.

Why do people change?

There is always a risk involved in changing because things may not turn out the way we want.

Changes in people don't usually occur immediately, big changes can occur when we plant an idea and allow the person to think about that idea. If we push it too much we get an argument against it because nobody likes change. If things are not causing us a big hassle, we want the situation to remain as it is because we are coping OK. On the other hand, we may want the things to change but if it is a toss-up between the devil we know and the devil we don't know, our fear of the unknown will win out.

The real changes in kids and other people will come about from them working out their own version of ideas, sometimes in the most unexpected way. A woman was telling me one day that she had heard me speak to a group about four years previously and that a remark I made 'saved her marriage'. Obviously it wasn't the remark that saved her marriage, she had a problem with her marriage and was genuinely looking for a solution to that problem. My remark simply triggered a train of thought in her and she examined her beliefs and values in the light of that train of thought.

We change when our behaviour causes us a problem

When we remember that all human behaviour is to satisfy our own needs and wants, it follows that we only change our behaviour when that behaviour becomes a problem to us in some way. In other words, if we can see there is a better way to get what we want, or what we are doing is not getting us what we want.

When we change what we're doing, it's because we think we'll miss out on something if we don't change. For example, people who are planning a holiday may suddenly start doing things for their neighbours, because the cat will need feeding while they're away.

Selfish? Yes, but there are times when we do something for someone because we feel good when they feel good and we give money to the Salvos and feel good about it, regardless of whether anyone knows about it or not. There are times when we do someone a favour so they 'owe us one'.

Kids change for the same reasons as adults change. They're trying hard to get what they need or want and if they can be shown a better way to get it they will probably change to that way. If they find their present behaviour is not succeeding, they will be more open to trying a different way.

If you want a child's behaviour to change, show them a better way of getting what they want so that if they continue to do what they are doing they are putting themselves at a disadvantage.

When a child is being irresponsible in the way he's trying to get something from you, there are two things you can do. First of all be sure that he knows a more responsible way and if he doesn't, teach him how. Secondly, once he knows a more responsible way to get what he wants, don't give him what he wants until he acts more responsibly.

Smoking and other drugs

Whenever I give a talk about changing behaviour, a question is always asked about getting kids to give up some drug or other. Drug addiction is a terrible thing and terrifies most parents. They nearly always have a dread of the illegal drugs and seem to scoff when told that alcohol and tobacco are the worst and most dangerous drugs, but it's true.

Partly because of it's danger and partly because nicotine addiction is possibly the hardest drug addiction to beat, I'll use smoking as an example of changing behaviour and of the special difficulties that young people are faced with in trying to 'kick the habit'.

I started smoking when I was nine years old and continued to smoke for thirty-nine years, with many attempts to quit along the way. Most long term smokers would have thought long and hard about quitting and would have tried many times and many ways to quit. Because it's so hard to do, many smokers eventually make a new year resolution to give up trying to quit smoking.

It's even harder for young people because in order to quit they have to be able to see the long term benefits that offset the immediate misery they would have to go through, and as we know from Chapters 1 and 2 young people have great difficulty seeing far into the future. Another thing making it hard for young people is the vague belief that the future is going to be the same as the present, therefore the misery they feel now is how they are always going to feel if they continue to do without the 'old coffin nail'. It is doubtful that anyone would commit themselves to a life of misery and that's how it looks to an adolescent who is faced with breaking their addiction.

Some people wrongly call it, 'Breaking the habit'. It's not a habit. It's an addiction. An addiction the kids probably started through a feeling of belonging to the peer group but peer pressure is no longer the reason, it's because they are straight out addicted.

"SO - YOU'VE STILL GOT A CIGARETTE PROBLEM?"
"YEAH - I'VE GOT TO DRESS UP LIKE THIS TO BUY A PACK!"

Because of all the above, the campaign against smoking has had little success with young people but has been very successful in changing the behaviour of adults.

Tobacco, alcohol and other drugs give teenagers escape from the pain of life, or ease it. Most will get control of their drug taking as they move to adult versions of social drug taking. However, some kids will get addicted to alcohol and other drugs. What can you do about it?

It is generally accepted that an alcoholic will not change until he admits he is an alcoholic and it is no different with the other drugs. The person has to own the problem as a problem and as theirs to solve. But that is not enough by itself because then they have to have the opportunity, the ability and the desire to change.

In other words, changing drug addiction behaviour is little different to trying to change other behaviour. The difference is that it is much harder to get the person to own the problem and to have the desire to change. We can help by giving the opportunity, which includes never encouraging them to continue with the drug in any way, and by making sure they know all the places and people they can get assistance from. Another way to help is to let them take the consequences of their behaviour and not be rescuing them, except when their behaviour is life threatening. Paying the rent for kids who spend their money on dope and alcohol is really only subsidising their drugs.

Accepting the past

We started off talking about what you wanted to change and we have looked at what you can change. We've also had a brief look at why people change their behaviour. An important thing about the present is that it is the result of everything that has happened in the past. In other words, it would be foolish not to learn from our past. We can't change it but it is a huge storehouse of knowledge to help us make responsible decisions *now*.

Do you know what you want to change? If you do, my next question is, 'Is what you are doing now moving you towards what you want or away from it?'

As we saw earlier, the past is dead and nothing can ever change it and yet we spend so much time wishing the past were different. The other source of trouble for us is the future; it is the source of our anxiety because everything we are anxious about is in the future. It may only be a few seconds into the future but it's still in the future. To make it a bit easier to read, and save me some typing, from now on I'm going to use 'now' to mean 'the present situation'.

I am about to say something very obvious. When the future that we were anxious about gets here, it becomes now. Wasn't that profound? The future that we worried about before has arrived so we worry about a new future. You probably think that's also a pretty obvious statement but here's the point: all we really have to worry about is that we act responsibly now, right now. We can't do anything about the past and when the future gets here it becomes now so if we act responsibly now we are also taking care of the future.

If you have decided what you want to change then all you have to do is decide whether what you are doing now is moving you closer to what you want or further away from it.

People who only concern themselves with acting responsibly now can change their world by changing *what* they are working towards or by changing *how* they are working towards it. The important part of this is always now because it is only now that we can do anything about the future.

Acceptance of the past is something that we all find hard but we can't really go forward until we accept that what is available in the present is all we really have to work with. To accept the past means to accept all the good things that have happened and all the bad and some people have been brutally treated and violated in the past. Some of these people take a long time to come to accept what has happened to them before they can move easily into the future.

People who have been sexually abused can find it very difficult to come to terms with what happened to them but when they can accept their own innocence, and the betrayal of trust, they can begin to adjust and move forward.

Accepting the past does not mean accepting the past as the way to go in the future, like one father who was losing the battle to control his kids. He had trouble understanding why any parent should change from a style they found worked every time in the past in getting quick results. 'A good thump has worked wonders ever since the kids were little and that's all that's missing now and if it wasn't for me crook back, that's what he'd get. That'd fix him. Besides, that's the way my parents treated me and it hasn't done me no harm, none of this mamby-pamby stuff.' He neglected to mention that maybe the boy now being a good 150 mm taller than him was a factor in not giving him a thump.

Accepting the past really means accepting the present situation and that includes your own good points and faults. It means looking at now and accepting that it is as it is, including what you can do and what you can't do.

Do you have one leg shorter than the other? OK, you have one leg shorter than the other and that's all it means. Everything else is in your mind and depends on how you react to having one leg shorter than the other.

Looking to the future

Now that you have decided what you want and you have looked at the present situation, I want to ask you a challenging question. What can you do right now to move a little closer to getting what you want? No, I didn't ask what you can't do and I didn't ask what you don't want to do, I asked what *can* you do?

Maybe you want to do something that seems out of reach but what can you do to get just a little closer to it? Once you have got that little closer, what can you do to get a little closer still? Now don't think of reasons why you can't do it, think about what you can do.

Maybe you have decided to adjust your parenting to take advantage of the children's natural tendency towards freedom by holding them responsible for negotiating limits and rules. In the past, too many parents looked to counsellors, doctors, psychologists, social workers, psychiatrists, teachers, youth workers and the local garbage collector to change the behaviour of the child, when the real solution was to put it back on the kids.

If this is what you say you want, then I ask that question again that challenges whether you are genuine when you say that's what you want. What can you do right now to move a little closer to getting what you want?

You may have tried this in the past but slipped back into old ways again. It's quite natural that we generally want to stick with what works for us and so we are no different from our kids when it comes to using tried and proven methods of solving our problems. We may try new ways but as soon as we get into the sticky bit we revert back to the old ways.

A child who is being taught to solve his problems without fighting may use peaceful methods until it looks like he's going to lose, then he throws a straight left, because that's always worked in the past. I don't see any difference in this to the parent who tries out a non-violent way of parenting but reaches for the wooden spoon when the child says 'no' for the second time.

The principle is the same, the old way gets sure and quick results for parents and for kids. Don't the kids learn it from the parents in the first place? I wonder how many times the not-so-funny scene has been played out of a parent giving a child a hiding for fighting. What sort of message is given to a child who is being beaten to teach him that using violence is not tolerated? Does the child take notice of the words or does he take notice of the blows that punctuate each word?

I sometimes squirm inside when I ask myself 'What can you do right now to move closer to getting what you want' because it really puts me on the spot to be honest about what I tell myself I want. Sometimes I'm not prepared to move closer to what I say I want and that makes it obvious that there is something more important that I would have to move further away from in order to get closer to what I say I want. In other words, there is a conflict of values or there is something I fear would happen if I made the move.

The question is a challenge but it's also very handy to help me work out my values and fears. The same thing applies in my work with kids, parents and other people. It can be used to help them work out their values and fears but unless I am willing to apply it to myself I don't think I have the right to apply it to other people, because it is a challenge.

When that question is asked, parents may start to talk about what sorts of things stop them, 'But I can't because...' 'I haven't got the money.' 'My friends would laugh at me.'

My reply would be, 'I asked you what you can do right now to move you a little closer to what you want, not what you can't do, or what's stopping you, what *can* you do?' Some kids will try again and again to put the attention on other people and things but it's important to keep bringing the attention back onto what they can do.

There is an old saying, 'Look where you're going or go where you're looking'. In other words, know where your behaviour is taking you or act in a way that will take you where you want to go. The first part of the saying means going along for the ride, the second part means that you can control where the ride is going.

The question, 'What can you do?' is a handy tool for teaching a child, or revealing to an adult, the use of what's here *now* to help them get what they want, that the decisions they make *now* will either help or hinder them getting what they want. But remember that any tool badly used can cause damage. Therefore, are you willing to apply this to yourself before we talk about applying it to your kids? If you do then you have more right to challenge your teenager. Example is always the best teacher.

One reason you should apply this question to yourself is so you can come to terms with your own excuses and attempts to blame other people and things, because we all do it to some extent. Practising on yourself can make you a bit more gentle and understanding in pushing to keep your child focused on what he can do, and less likely to 'rubbish' the child for his attempts to say why he can't do it.

You can be gentle and understanding and still not allow yourself to be sidetracked by attempts to move your attention onto other things, or attempts to get you to make suggestions.

Putting up with short term unpleasantness for long term gain

Parents often say they do things they don't want to do. That is not really true. We may want things to be different but either we don't know how to change it or we don't want to put up with the immediate unpleasantness of changing.

Example 1

(Memories from the past)
A small child will not go to sleep at night and cries tears of misery unless the parent stays in the room. If it was all totalled up, the parent spends many hours pacifying the child and the child spends many hours crying. Whenever a decision is made to let the kid cry, the parent feels guilt and anguish while the child is crying, and may have vague fears that the child will be resentful, and this leads to giving in and pacifying the child. However, most parents discover that there are usually two nights of crying, say three hours in total, before the child is broken out of the habit and that three hours of crying and anguish brings peace for both in the long run.

Example 2

A teenager becomes verbally abusive and insulting whenever the parent refuses to give her money for cigarettes. The parent wants the relationship to be different and knows that giving in to her will mean damage to the kid's health. She also knows the child will abuse her again and again to get her own way but the immediate unpleasantness is not worth going through so the money is handed over. To get through this one, the parent would need to take a chance and be assertive.

I don't have the patience

Many people say they haven't got the patience to put up with the child's behaviour and will say that things counsellors advise them to do only work for a little while or they only tried it for a little while and it didn't work.

They claim they don't have the patience, never did have it and can't develop it. Some will proudly attribute this to a family failing, because their parents were the same and it's unfair to expect them to be any different. This seems to be some sort of excuse that should be accepted as explaining why there is no sense in them trying.

However, I firmly believe that if there was a million dollar offer made for people who could develop a certain level of patience, there would be many, many people impatiently clamouring to do courses to learn patience. The long term ability of children to solve their problems or to cope better with their lives is worth more than a million dollars and may set a new tradition for the family.

Now we are ready to apply all this to the kids.

Things to think about

✔ The child's 'faults' you want to change now may be her strengths in the future.

✔ Past events cannot be changed and must be accepted before we can make the changes we want in the present.

✔ You can change your immediate world by changing your own behaviour.

✔ To change behaviour requires accepting ownership of the problem in question, and the desire to change.

✔ What do you want to change now? What can you do now to move closer to what you want?

✔ Short term unpleasantness is well worth enduring to achieve behaviour changes beneficial for parents and children in the future.

CHAPTER 11

Introducing Teenagers to Reality

The reality questions

THE THREE QUESTIONS mentioned here are derived from Dr William Glasser's 'Reality Therapy' and in this chapter we are going to apply this to the kids.

Reality is *now*. This is one of the things kids have right, and they delight in telling parents to 'get real'. Well, it's time the parents showed kids what being real is all about, to introduce them to reality. See, you feel better already, just knowing it could be possible to do such a thing.

A large number of questions and statements can be used to bring reality to the kids and these can be divided into three groups. How many questions and statements are in each group depends only on your imagination, so you can think up as many questions and statements as you like.

The first group is about, 'What do you want?' This seems like a simple and innocent question but used in the right way it becomes a tool to help a child become a responsible person. It helps a child to feel important, can build up her self-esteem and, in conjunction with two other questions, can be used to put a child in charge of her future; to give her confidence to take control of her life and responsibility for her own behaviour. Not bad for such an innocent looking question.

The second group is about, 'What are you doing?' Another simple question that can be used to get children to do a bit of self-judgement about their behaviour and whether what they say they want and what they are doing match up. Parents don't have to judge a child's behaviour, get the child to judge her own behaviour. She will be harder on herself than you would.

" *YOU'RE GOING OUT LIKE THAT ? .. COME ON GUYS—GET REAL !* "

The third group is about, 'What can you do?' This question is the real challenge to kids and to people of all ages to, behaviour-wise, put up or shut up. To bring their behaviour into line with their stated aims or come clean on what their real aims are. It also puts the responsibility squarely with the young person to be responsible for herself.

Before we go on to look at the three groups of questions, there is something I want to impress on you. So far I have suggested that you externalise things like rules, limits, traditional parenting, hand-me-down beliefs and values, and problems. However, the one thing that you should not externalise and not allow your children to learn to externalise, is the responsibility for the effects of behaviour.

Part of facing reality is to face the reality that we are responsible for our own behaviour, for our own choices. Our children are also responsible for their behaviour, for the choices they make in how they act. That is a frightening thought in some ways but when we remember that as long as we concentrate on acting responsibly *now* there is no problem with it. I am happier being held responsible for something I can control rather than for something I can't control. I can control what I do but I can't control what my kids do.

We will now look at the variations of the three questions but remember that all questions can be changed to statements if asking questions causes a problem.

What do you want?

There are many variations of the question, 'What do you want?' and these are some of them. (Remember, these are variations of one question. It is not suggested that you ask them all in the one talk, unless you want to wreck the relationship.)

■ What are your plans?
■ Where are you going?
■ What's your goal?
■ What do you want to do?
■ What are your aims and objectives?
■ Where do you want to be at?
■ What is important to you?
■ Who would you like to meet?
■ What do you hope to gain?
■ Where are you heading?
■ What's in it for you?

Kids often answer this question with a 'don't want' instead of a want. Don't wants are not allowed. We only deal in wants, aims, goals, objectives, needs and targets. This means that a don't want has to be turned into a want. To do this you could be direct and say, 'That's what you don't want but I asked you what you do want'.

Another way is for you to change the reply around so that it is seen as a want. The child says, 'I don't want any limits put on me'. The parent replies, 'I take that to mean that you want to have more say in the rules of this house'.

A second question can be used to find a want; as usual the child says what he doesn't want, 'I don't want to go to school'. How do you change that into a want? Ask him another question like, 'Alright, if you weren't going to school, what would you have gained?' His reply might be, 'My freedom'. You then have the want that you were looking for and can bring this out with, 'So what you really want is to feel free from the hassles at school?' 'Yeah', says the child. Mother can then become helpful, 'Well, let's have a look at those hassles'.

There are many times when the situation is so delicate that you want to avoid pushing her for an answer or when the child makes it hard by refusing to tell what she wants. There are times when it is best to leave her alone because expecting kids to sit and have a talk about their problems and long term goals can create problems. Parents may think a child who won't tell them what she intends to do in the long term doesn't trust them or maybe that the child is aimless.

It's unreasonable to expect a child to sit down and have a 'meaningful talk' with someone unless they feel at ease with that person. Besides, there are some things the kids don't want to talk to their parents about no matter how well they get along. Your kids might confide in the neighbour and the neighbour's kids might confide in you.

Practice at setting and achieving goals comes in the small things, the little wants of daily living. Deciding that I want to go down the street, or I want to save twenty dollars this month, or I want to impress someone, or I want to join a basketball team, or I want sausages for dinner. If you want your kids to tell you their wants and their plans, listen to the little plans and treat them as important. A parent who doesn't listen to a kid's little plans won't get the chance to hear her big ones.

When a child is at ease talking to you about small things, she is more likely to risk telling you about something more important and that may happen quite suddenly and unexpectedly. If you're not in the habit of listening to her small talk and treating it as important, you will probably miss out on being told the 'deep and meaningfuls'.

What are you doing?

Here are some of the variations of the question, 'What are you doing?'

■ What is the rule about it?
■ What are you doing to get it?
■ What's the present situation?
■ What are all the conditions at the moment?

- Where are we at?
- Is what you're doing now moving you closer to what you want or further away?
- Do you know a better way to get what you want?
- What led to this situation?
- What do other people say about it?
- What do other people suggest you do?
- How do other people handle it?
- What are your feelings about it?
- What are your beliefs about it?
- Are you pleased with the way you are acting to get what you want?
- Do you have enough knowledge to get what you want?
- Do you have the opportunity to get what you want?
- What are the obstacles you have to get over?
- Who are the people who are willing to help you?
- Who are the people working against you?
- Who are the people who will be affected?
- What effect are you having on other people?
- What do you need to be able to do it?

This question urges a child to look at their present behaviour and to judge for themselves whether it is responsible or not. Its many variations are used to explore the present situation, what is here and now, what is real. Those questions are used to get the child to know all the information available in order for her to make an informed decision about getting what she wants.

The parent is not around all the time to be telling the child what is responsible behaviour and what isn't but the parent can give a child guidelines of responsible behaviour to carry around with her all her life by getting the child to judge her own behaviour in regard to what she wants and considering the needs of others. If she is used to judging her own performance, there is no need for you to do anything except be there when she wants to talk about a problem.

What can you do?

Here are some of the variations of the question, 'What can you do?'

- How do you think you can achieve what you want?

- How do you clear the way to get there?
- What are your options?
- Which option have you chosen?
- What can you do right now to move you a little closer to getting what you want?
- What can we do?
- What do you think you could handle right now?
- Which way would get you there the quickest?
- What would be the outcome of doing it that way?
- Which way are you going to go?
- What is the first step in your plan?
- What do you see as the first thing to do?
- What are you going to do first?

The 'what can you do?' group of questions keeps the attention focused on the future and getting the child to realise that she can solve her own problems. This group explores the possible ways the problem can be solved and encourages the child to achieve her aims, to take steps towards what she wants.

Remember, we are not talking about big plans. We are talking about little everyday wants and needs. All human behaviour has a purpose and this group of questions helps to clear up what the purpose of a child's behaviour is. The behaviour will be towards the real purpose and the child is encouraged to judge whether her real purpose is what she thought it was, by whether she is prepared to take the steps towards that. In other words, whether she is prepared to match up her words and her actions.

Kids will generally want to tell you what they can't do but 'can't do' is to be treated the same as 'don't want'. A can't do has to be turned into a can do. 'That's what you can't do but I want to know what you can do'.

If a child insists that he really doesn't know how or where to start then the first step for her is to find out, so the next question would be, 'Who could you find out from?'

Quite often a child will have more than one want and become confused because he is not prepared to work towards what he says he wants. The reason being that to work towards that want means moving away from another want, one that he may not even be aware of because it is just 'there'.

Building self-esteem

One of the basic needs of humans is to feel important, to belong and to feel loved. These three things are interconnected because they make up the general feeling a person has about themselves that we call 'self-esteem'. Good self-esteem is having a good feeling about yourself in relation to other people and the world. Low self-esteem is having a bad feeling about yourself in relation to other people and the world.

The basic human need is for self-esteem, to like oneself, to be able to live with oneself. All social feeling, all feelings of belonging, all the capacity to love others depends on this. Life without self-esteem is not worth living.

We often hear or read about people who we believe 'should' have high self-esteem – 'pop' stars, movie stars, successful business people – who leave suicide notes that reveal their very low self-esteem. This brings home to me that things like good looks or particular talents don't rate much when it comes to how we feel about ourselves. Self-esteem is something that has been built up over the years from the response of other people to what a child does, from the thousand or more times a day people show their approval or disapproval of her actions.

Quite often the bad image we have of ourselves as adults comes from things said to us when we were kids, things that belittle us in some way, the effects of which have stayed with us ever since.

The self-esteem of a child who has always seemed self-confident can suddenly become very delicate when she gets to adolescence. It is a time when children feel unsure, unsafe, and 'different'.

Adults tend to tell kids how they should feel, as if what the child actually feels is ridiculous and only shows how silly she is. That doesn't do much to boost the kid's self-esteem.

It doesn't matter how other people think the child should feel, the only thing that matters is that the child feels insignificant, unloved and alone. Loneliness, being cut off, being different, and having no control are all genuine feelings that young people can feel very intensely and it's no good telling a kid that she 'has every reason to feel good about herself' when the cold, hard fact is, she doesn't feel good about herself and to a young person this condition will never end.

The lucky ones amongst us have the opportunity to be around those who make us feel important and needed, those who accept us and respect us. Kids want the same and this is one of the many reasons they spend so much time with their peer group. Their friends usually make them feel accepted and important and this is sometimes responded to by believing themselves to be deeply in love.

Parents can become good at boosting a child's self-esteem. How? Simply by using the many variations of the three questions and statements mentioned above. The reason you can boost a child's self-esteem is that every time you speak or act towards a child, or anyone for that matter, you give them an underlying message and the underlying message of these three questions can be that the child is important to you.

As we saw in Chapter 7, however, the message given depends not on the words but on the way they are said. If used in a demanding, impatient, 'you're mad' way, the hidden message is the opposite to the messages given below and will damage the self-esteem. How are *you* going to use these questions? Look again at the question you just read and ignore that the word 'you' is emphasised, does it change the message of the question?

Separating the behaviour from the child

One reason the use of the three groups of questions works to boost self-esteem is because they help to separate the child from the behaviour. The attention is always on the behaviour and not on the person, so that what the child is doing can be examined without judging the child.

Kids usually don't mind giving a description of what happened when asked a question from the second group like, 'What happened?' but will clam up if asked, 'Why did you do that?'

If it is necessary to devalue a child's behaviour, there must be a clear distinction made between the child and the behaviour so the child can be shown to be important. At the same time, there must be a clear message to the child that there is no separation of the child from the responsibility for the effects of the behaviour. The child is the one who did it and the child is the one who has to be held responsible for the effects of that behaviour.

Total disapproval of behaviour, without going on and on about it, is a severe consequence in itself and it can be done without harming self-esteem, as long as there is no put down of the person. It's important, though, for you to let

" O.K. – HOW MUCH IS THIS SELF ESTEEM... ERR..
.. NEW GYM SHOES GOING TO COST ME ? "

the child know that you are willing to discuss the behaviour, and why it is so unacceptable to you, anytime the child chooses. Total disapproval must only be used for serious things because it loses its meaning if used for every little thing.

Whenever the attention is taken off the behaviour, by sending the parent on a guilt trip, or distracting attention onto the behaviour of other kids, or any other way, the behaviour goes unexamined and may be forgotten.

Children look for ways to justify their behaviour or to take attention away from their bad behaviour. They refuse to take responsibility for bad behaviour because this makes them less than perfect, something they don't want to be reminded about. Therefore, kids will jump at the opportunity to divert attention onto anything rather than have it focused on their behaviour. The attempt to divert attention is less likely to happen if the behaviour is separated from the child.

We use questions to gain information but we can frame those questions to stimulate the development of children and increase their self-esteem. A wonderful effect is that we cannot do this without at the same time boosting our own self-esteem. What we do for and to other people, we do to ourselves. So do yourself a favour by practising asking questions in a way that shows a high level of interest, concern, respect and consideration for your child.

This can be difficult if the young person's present behaviour is absolutely obnoxious and you don't even want to know him let alone show respect. I'm not saying it's easy, parents have the hardest job on earth, but try to hate the behaviour while showing love and respect for the child who is behaving that way.

Using 'What do you want?' to build self-esteem

The underlying message of this group of questions is:

> *I like to hear what is important to you to achieve in ordinary everyday living because what is important to you is important to me. It doesn't have to be big plans or dreams, just the little things that you need or want. I want you to be always gaining something and that is why I sometimes change the wording to turn it into something you are reaching for. This way you will be a winner because you will always be looking ahead to what you can gain rather than looking behind to what you want to avoid.*

If this is the attitude you have when you are talking about what the young person wants then that will be the hidden message. Your attitude comes through no matter how hard you try to hide it.

Using 'What are you doing?' to build self-esteem

The underlying message of this group of questions is:

> *Because you are so important to me I will do everything I can to help you to act responsibly. When you are not acting responsibly I will not allow you to sidetrack me or distract my attention away from what you want because what you want is important to me. Therefore, it is important for you to look at what you are doing in order to judge if your actions are helping you get what you want or not. You do know responsible ways of getting what you want and you are capable of judging your own behaviour, with regard to considering the needs of others. Because acting responsibly lifts you up and acting irresponsibly weakens you, I will not do you harm by accepting behaviour that you know is irresponsible.*

If this is the attitude that you have when you're talking about what the young person is doing or what's led up to the present situation, then the above will be the hidden message. There is no blame, no finding of fault. You are not judging the child but there is a strong focus on the child examining her own behaviour and judging it for herself. However, you are judging whether the child knows a responsible way to get what she wants, so you can teach her if she doesn't know how to act, but generally if kids want something badly enough they know how to behave.

Using 'What can you do?' to build self-esteem

The underlying message in this group of questions is:

I am confident in your ability to run your own life and make your own decisions. You can get what you want because you have the ability to think up alternative plans. You can choose between the different ways of doing things and are responsible when it comes to consequences.

If this is the attitude that you have when you are talking to an adolescent about the future, you are empowering her to meet her troubles and solve problems. You would be challenging her to move towards her goals, to keep her face forward, to be a winner. Any person constantly treated as a winner would seldom, if ever, need to be told they are important because they would *feel* important.

Just telling a child he is loved or important is not enough for him to feel loved or important. A few years ago, the father of one of our male residents paid a rare visit to his son. The boy was excited to see him but was quickly deflated when his father told him, 'I love you, son, but now that I've remarried there is no longer any room for you in my life'. When I tried to salvage something from the situation he went further and said there was not even any physical room in his house where the kid could sleep if he visited, not even on the floor or on a couch – nowhere. Not surprisingly, the kid fell apart soon after that and took to drugs. He disappeared after a while and I lost track of him.

This reminded me of a text somewhere in the Bible that says something like, 'Those who have much shall receive even more while those who have little will have what little they have taken from them'. This can be so true when it comes to self-esteem.

Becoming a 'self-esteem service station'

Kids and other people get their self-esteem battered about sometimes and they head for places and people who help them feel good again. Remember when the kids used to run in to get their mortal wounds kissed better and then rush out into the world again? It's the same thing now, just different sized kids.

You can become a 'self-esteem service station' for your children by being there when they hurt and at the same time boost your own self-esteem. Boosting someone's self-esteem can be a self-centred act because when we set out to boost the self-esteem of another person we look at what we have done and have a good feeling about ourselves: we boost our own self-esteem. Therefore the more we act to boost another person, the more we boost ourselves.

I have heard many parents say, 'It's too late to be doing all this with my kids' but it's never too late to boost someone up. The past is gone and you can't do anything about it. The time to start being a self-esteem service station is *now* because there is no way we can start yesterday. Don't use yesterday as an excuse for doing nothing today.

" *THANKS MUM.. I NEEDED A TOP-UP....* "

Everyday reality of problem solving

It's time that we put the reality idea together with the idea that whoever does the approaching is the one who owns the problem. Mixed with this is the parent's resistance to allowing themselves to be distracted from concentrating on the child's wants, present behaviour, and possible ways of getting what he wants.

I will dissect the first example and let you do the same to the two following examples.

Example 1

'The approach'
Son (calling out): Mum?

First reality question that asks about his need or want:

Mum: What do you want?

'The problem'
Son: I want to go down the street.

Second reality question that clearly sets out whose problem it is and asks him to look at whether his present behaviour is helping him get what he wants or hindering him:

Mum: What are you doing about it?

Son ignores the invitation to examine his behaviour and gives his quickie solution:

Son: You can drive me there.

Mother's reply that shows a willingness to help but sets limits because of her own needs:

Mum: I'm busy cooking for about an hour but will be happy
                 to drive you down then.

Son (protesting): But that's no good, I want to go now.

Mother restates the limits and puts the onus back onto him to think up ways to solve his problem:

| Mum: | Well, I can do it for you in an hour. What ways can you think of to get you there quicker? |

Son resorts to a tried and proven method of getting his own way – send Mother on a guilt trip:

| Son: | But that'll be too late and I'll be the only one of my whole group to miss out, just because you won't take five minutes to drive me there. |

Mother no longer falls for this and again puts it back on to him:

| Mum: | Does blaming me get you down the street any sooner? |

Son now decides to increase pressure for a guilt trip because it has always worked:

| Son: | What sort of a Mother are you that doesn't care enough about my feelings and my needs to even take five minutes of your precious time to help me. I always thought Mothers were supposed to love their kids but you don't give a stuff about me do you? |

Mother doesn't take any of the baits that he throws out but sticks to the original problem:

| Mum: | The important thing for you right now is how you are going to get down the street to do what you want to do, now that you know it will be an hour before I can take you there. Let me know if you want any help in thinking of another way to solve your problem.' |

The son may then storm out and either discover he has things called legs or jump on his bike and get some exercise.

The other thing he may do is become more angry and if this happens it may be better for Mother to withdraw from the situation by refusing to be drawn any further into the discussion, while at the same time keeping very friendly and calm. Maybe even with the occasional 'dear' or 'sweetheart' thrown in if that's the normal way Mother speaks to the child.

Another way could be for Mother to slip out into the garden or maybe go to another part of the house to put some distance between herself and the angry child so that when he makes another approach by calling out, Mother can cheerfully answer, 'Be there in a minute, dear, what do you want?' (A return to the first reality question.)

There could be different endings to this:

> Son (muttering): Ah nothing, get stuffed! He walks out.
>
> Mum: Have a good time dear! See you at teatime.

Or as a last ditch attempt:

> Son (calling out): I'm going now and I'm never coming back.
>
> Mum: What was that dear? Oh, you're going are you? See you at teatime then. Have a good time'.

Or maybe the son will simply call out, 'What time do I have to be home then?'

Mother's reply could be, 'The usual time dear, five o'clock'.

During all of this no power struggle has been allowed to develop. Mother has stayed firmly in control of her parenting by helping the child to own his problem and to solve it, while at the same time showing him that he and his problems are important, too important to waste time by getting into a fight.

Now it's your turn. Let's have a look at another one but this time you can do the analysis of what's happening and how Mother handles it.

Example 2

John sweetly attracts Mum's attention with his usual, 'Mum?'

And gets the usual response, 'Yes, John, what do you want?'

'My sports shoes are worn out and I want a pair of Reeboks', he says.

Mother is cautious about accepting this at face value, 'When do you need the shoes by?' she asks.

John doesn't hear the cautious tone in her voice and thinks he's on a winner. 'Before sports next Wednesday, Mum'.

Mum decides to accept responsibility for supplying John's shoes but just can't afford expensive shoes. 'I'll get you some sports shoes by next sports day but I can't afford Reeboks, it will have to be the regular sports shoes', she states.

John doesn't want to accept this: 'But I want Reebocks, the others all suck, nobody wears them anymore'.

Mother knows from experience that she loses if she enters into an argument with John, so she states what her position is, 'You want new sports shoes and I can only afford the regular type of shoe. If you want more expensive shoes, what are you doing about making up the difference?'

John replies, quick as a flash, 'You get me the Reebocks and I'll pay you back later'.

However Mother has been caught by this one before, so she says: 'The last time we had that arrangement you didn't pay me back so I think you can get the money first and then I'll put in the price of the regular shoes'.

Now John tries the old guilt trip method, 'Oh, that's lovely that is. Just because I forgot to pay you once you don't trust me and will hold it against me for the rest of my life. You always say people should forgive and forget but it doesn't apply to you does it?. Besides, that's in the past, and how do you know I haven't changed if you don't give me a chance.'

Mother has been down that track before but knows if she gets sucked in she will regret it later. She surprises herself a little by sticking to what she had said, 'I have said what I'm prepared to do. What other ways are open to you to get the money before next sports day, so you can have what you want?'

John starts to think that things are getting a bit tough, so he tries another method, mixing fear with guilt: 'I could steal the money I s'pose. The clothes in the lockers at the stadium are always an easy way to get money. If I'm caught it'll be your fault our name becomes dirt around the town and I'll never be able to get a decent job'.

Mother is afraid of this but knows that if she gives in now he will be able to blackmail her every time he wants something, 'Yes, that is one way, John, that I hope you don't decide on, but it really is up to you. I would be very unhappy to see you getting into trouble for deciding to steal money but if that's what you decide to do I'll have to respect your decision'.

John decides it isn't going to work and becomes a bit more reasonable, 'Well, how else can I get the money before next week?'

This gives Mother an opportunity to help John explore options that are open to him now that he has accepted responsibility for the problem but she decides to give him a little time to think about it: 'What if we both think about it for now and we'll put our ideas together at teatime tonight'. John hesitates for a moment but then grunts agreement.

This third example is one where the parent wants to approach the child and includes turning a 'don't want' into a 'want'.

Example 3

Daughter, Joan, is obviously unhappy and her behaviour is causing others in the house to be unhappy.

Father realises she has a problem and that it's her problem to solve but as a parent he wants to help. And besides, he wants to have a peaceful home for all and Joan is not handling her problem very well. This in itself is a problem because it means she is trying to bring attention to what's bothering her but at the same time will probably say she doesn't want any help with it.

Father approaches with the usual attention getter, 'Joan?' and Joan is as cheerful as she has been lately and snaps, 'Yeah, waddayawan?'

Father isn't put off by her mood and admits that he owns his problem, 'I'm concerned that you appear to be unhappy about something and that unhappiness is affecting everyone in the house. I would like to help if I can'.

Just as he expected, Joan says, 'It's my problem and it doesn't affect you or anyone else. I'll work it out for myself.'

Father is affected and says so, 'I agree that you are the one who has to solve your own problems, and I respect that, but this time your unhappiness is affecting others and it seems you're having trouble working it out. Maybe if you tell me about it we can work it out together.'

Joan hesitates but then blurts it out: 'I don't want to go with Jimmy anymore'.

Father believes people are happier working towards something rather than avoiding something, so he turns it around to be a 'want' instead of a 'don't want', 'You want to change the relationship with Jimmy. What sort of a relationship do you want to change it to?'

Joan is a bit surprised at this change in the problem but replies: 'Well, I still want to be friends with him, he's a nice guy'.

Instead of the 'what are you doing' question Father says, 'What ways have you thought of so far?'

Joan outlines all the ways she has thought of but is obviously unhappy with these alternatives. Each way involves explanations as to her reasons for breaking it off, and she knows Jimmy will be hurt no matter which way she does it.

Father suggests, 'Maybe another way would be to simply tell him the bare facts, that you no longer want a girlfriend/boyfriend relationship but you do want to be friends. To just make it as simple and as clear as possible and then stick to that.'

This gives Joan another alternative that she may choose, or that she may think about and alter to suit herself.

Things to think about

✔ When discussing a child's needs, asking the 'reality' questions 'What do you want?', 'What are you doing?' and 'What can you do?' is useful for avoiding parent/child power struggles, boosting the child's self-esteem, and encouraging him towards responsible behaviour.

✔ These questions are important tools for separating the behaviour from the child and so protect her self-esteem.

✔ They can also convey love and care to enhance the child's feelings of importance and belonging.

CHAPTER 12

Punishment

What it means

L EARNING IS A LIFETIME job and none of us will ever know every-thing about anything. There is a great deal still to know about how to handle difficult behaviour but the remaining chapters will be talking about what parents have done and can do when a child's behaviour is unacceptable.

I believe very strongly that children must be disciplined and I argue for parents to make sure the kids are held responsible for what they do and there-fore take the consequences of what they do. I also argue that punishment should be avoided as much as possible in disciplining children.

To me, the word 'punishment' means: The inflicting of physical, psycho-logical, emotional, social, economical or spiritual pain.

Times change. What was considered good parenting a few years ago may be termed child abuse and so many people are confused about what they can and cannot do in trying to discipline kids.

Ridicule, put downs, smacking, pushing, name-calling and hitting are looked upon as evidence of child abuse. So is the failure to provide adequate food, clothing, shelter, love, education and things that are considered to be essential for a child's general development. It is also becoming accepted by some that denying a child the right to privacy, to choose their own friends, to read and watch what they like can be abuse.

There has been a great deal of publicity given to child abuse through the abuse of parental power, and to children being the victims of poor parenting and bad discipline methods. That publicity is justified because the amount of physical abuse is staggering, the amount of sexual abuse is frightening, and the number of times that both parents are involved in continuing this abuse goes against our usual beliefs about parental love.

There is a temptation for me to go on with stories of broken bones, the bruising, the rapes, the brutal treatment of kids by those who are supposed to be providing them with care and protection but this is not that sort of book.

I don't believe that this book will reach those people because they don't usually seek this sort of help, but I do believe that all of us have to be aware of our potential to abuse children. Whenever we have power we have the potential to abuse that power and parents have tremendous power over their children. Therefore parents have the potential to do tremendous damage to their children through abuse of that power.

The potential to abuse children is increased in many of us because we have been trained to use punishment in trying to make kids behave responsibly.

Punishment 'gets results' in changing behaviour

The positive side to punishment is that it gets quick results and everyone is looking for a quick fix. Everything is quick. Quick returns on investments, quick turnover, instant results, time is money. In these days of instant everything a long drawn out solution is not popular, even if that solution can be shown to have better long term benefits.

Back in the days when slaves were used to row the big galley ships, they rowed till they dropped and when the ship was going into battle they rowed faster and faster. They didn't row because of their love for the ships' owners or out of loyalty to the shipping company. They rowed because of the man who walked up and down whipping those who slackened off. If he wasn't there to whip them, the pace would soon slow and if they could get free from their chains they would probably kill him. The slaves would not see the whipping as a consequence for getting tired muscles and it would not change their beliefs about their loyalty to the boss. They would only work to avoid the punishment and only work while the punishment was there.

Some reasons against the use of punishment

There are short term benefits to using punishments in trying to manage mis-behaviour but there are many reasons why punishment should not be used. Some of those reasons will be mentioned under separate headings but just in case some get lost in the reading, the following list gives them in point form. No doubt there are other reasons but these will do for starters.

The use of punishment:

■ Takes the attention off the behaviour
■ Teaches kids to be irresponsible
■ Rescues the child from other consequences
■ Teaches the use of abuse and violence to solve problems
■ Prevents the child from gaining self-control and independence
■ Damages the relationship
■ Is likely to perpetuate the behaviour it tried to stop
■ Only works while punishment is there
■ Starts the child on the road to murder or self mutilation/suicide.

Punishment takes the attention off the behaviour

One effect of punishment is that punishment takes the attention off the behaviour. A whole book could be written on this aspect of punishment and the tricks that kids, and people in general, will get up to in order to keep attention off their misbehaviour.

The most important point in this section is this: If a child (or any other person) can keep attention off their behaviour they don't have to face up to being responsible for that behaviour.

The greatest help a parent can give their child along the road to responsible adulthood is to get them to look at their behaviour and how it is affecting themselves and other people.

Punishment takes the child's attention off the behaviour and puts it on a multitude of other things. The parent's right to punish; the size of the punishment; how the parent found out; the evidence; whether the parents had ever done that themselves; whether the parent can make it stick; and finally, whether the parent-child relationship is strong enough for the child to give in and accept the punishment.

Far better for the attention to be left on what the kid did and what effects it had on themselves and other people. Maybe they would come to understand why people become unhappy with that behaviour and how it reflects back on them in the way people treat them.

Punishment rescues the child from other consequences

Punishment is a form of rescuing, which can result in the child growing up the opposite of what the parent wanted.

Punishment is mostly used to teach the child to be a responsible adult. However, if what I am saying is true and punishment is a form of rescuing then the use of punishment is rescuing the young person from experiencing the natural or logical social consequences of his behaviour and is actually teaching him to be irresponsible. He starts to believe that it is the responsibility of other people to stop him from doing the wrong thing. He can do as he likes and leave it up to other people to control him.

The other thing he learns from this is not to get caught. A child who says she is not going to get into trouble any more may well mean that she is not going to get caught next time. The only time she gets into trouble is when she gets caught so it's simple logic to believe that the only thing she did wrong was to get caught.

Some kids in early adolescence believe that it is the parent's responsibility to stop them from doing the wrong thing and it is the parent's fault when they get into trouble through the parent failing to stop them. If these things are not corrected by them maturing or by the parent's discipline methods, they may

"NO, NO... I'LL TURN MY RADIO DOWN .... PROMISE ... "

grow up to add to the number of 'innocent' people who seem to fill our gaols; those who believe that it is society's job to stop them and the only thing they did wrong was to get caught.

It follows from all this that punishment prevents the child from gaining self-control and becoming an independent adult.

For example, a child gets a smack on the hand to stop him from touching something hot, but how is he ever going to learn what 'hot' means if he never gets to feel it? (Obviously you would not let a child get burnt learning what it means but he can learn these things under controlled conditions.) The point is that the punishment was put in place of whatever was the natural consequence of the behaviour: the child was rescued.

Punishment teaches the use of abuse and violence to solve problems

A good quick smack across the bum will fix the problem so that's what we do, even though we may be aware that we are giving the example that violence is acceptable in solving problems. Besides, we can't stand to be defied because we must have control and we can go into a blind rage if confronted with a child who challenges our position.

There is no doubt that punishment brings quick, noticeable results. Right up to recent years, I still believed in giving children a smack for misbehaviour and I had certainly given mine many a smack when they were little. One day my eldest son was mildly misbehaving in church and I smacked him on the bare thigh. Because of the way it was delivered, the sound of the smack was far louder than the force of the blow but it seemed that every kid in the church behaved themselves for the rest of the service.

Now, after seeing the misery that violent problem solving causes in families, I believe that any form of abuse in disciplining children should be avoided. With my grandchildren I set myself the challenge that violence is not an option for discipline. I don't pretend that I don't feel like giving them a good smack sometimes, just as I have often felt like thumping some of the teenagers I work with. At the same time, there are many parents I've felt like thumping too.

I don't let the kids get away with much but I make sure that I say what I mean and mean what I say. In other words, I am always able and willing to carry out what I say I intend to do about their misbehaviour. They cannot defy what I say I intend to do because I have control over what I say I will do.

If it were true that punishment or pain would deter a person from doing something, no child would learn to climb stairs because I think it likely that every baby who has learnt to climb stairs has done so after repeated failures that produced painful results.

Many people believe that a smack on the bottom doesn't harm a child and I suppose I would be hard put to prove that it does do harm. I also realise that many of the people who read this book believe in smacking a child as a form of discipline. I used to believe that a 'loving smack' on the bottom or back of the legs did no harm and was preferable to the child coming to some harm.

I can't prove smacking is harmful but I believe it teaches a child that violence is the thing to use when you want your own way with someone weaker than yourself. If the other person is stronger, make yourself stronger by whatever means you can. In short, smacking teaches a kid that if you want quick results, 'smack 'em out'.

Wanting smacking banned is not a popular stand to take because of the number of parents who still see it as the best and quickest way of getting and keeping control of the children.

However, parents of 2-to-4-year-olds soon learn that smacking does not stop their child from misbehaving; he may ignore or even laugh at the smack and continue with the unwanted behaviour. The smack then has to become a beating to have effect. With some, it gets to the stage that a beating is ignored. What do you do then?

The ultimate use of punishment to solve problems is capital punishment, against someone else (murder) or against the self (suicide). Too dramatic? I don't think so. Once we have started a child on the violence road we have no control over how far he is going to go down that road when faced with a big problem. What do you do to stop them going further down that road than you did? Smack 'em out? Better to show them another road that leads to what they want.

Biblical quotes are often used to justify the use of punishment and beatings in disciplining children. 'Spare the rod and spoil the child' is probably the most common one. People tend to use biblical sayings in a literal way when they are convenient for their argument but will say they're only symbolic if the literal interpretation doesn't suit them. The 'rod' could mean 'the punishment', or it could mean 'the load', or it could just as easily mean 'the consequence'.

Many violent people have told me how, 'I was given a smack across the ear whenever I stepped out of line and it didn't do me any harm'. The fact is that kids are hitting back, some physically, some by open rebellion or by walking out of the relationship. They have quite rightly been taught not to take abuse but at the same time have unfortunately been taught to use violence themselves.

Some parents are battling against a long tradition of using punishment on the kids. Their own grandparents and parents are sometimes putting pressure on young parents to use some 'good old-fashioned discipline' on the kids. The sort of parenting that worked for them in keeping the kids in line was fine then but is not fine now. Time changes all things and, like it or not, those methods are no longer acceptable.

Punishment prevents a child from gaining self-control and independence

Even when punishment works it does harm. The person who hands out the rewards and punishments is trying to be in charge of the child's life.

The kid does not learn the normal consequences of behaviour if there is an artificial reward or punishment being handed out. The person who does the handing out has control over the good things that happen and the bad things. The child is supposed to learn good behaviour this way but what happens when the 'rewarder' isn't around? Just like the slave in the galley ship, the good behaviour may stop because rewards and punishments are just different parts of the same thing and the actions and reactions of people are similar for both.

Relying on a reward and punishment system is fine when training animals but not kids. Kids need to learn self-control, to govern their own behaviour regardless of someone handing out rewards and punishments.

Punishment damages the relationship

Earlier I mentioned the slaves rowing the boat as an example of punishment working only while the man could use the whip and what could happen if he lost it. Most parents don't have an actual whip to lose but they can lose their authority over the kids, by the kids using the word 'no'.

When talking with parents about consequences, discipline or punishment, anything to do with the child keeping to the rules of the house, I often ask the question:

What would you do if your teenager said, 'No'?

If I want a more dramatic effect with some people I change it to:

What would you do if your teenager said, 'Get stuffed, do it yourself', when you tell him to do something?

If you haven't had this experience then just for a moment try to imagine yourself suddenly faced with that situation. How would you react? Would you have to 'get on top of him'? Would you back off but really let him know what you think of him?

What are you going to do if he refuses to get into the car when you try to bring him home from the street? Are you going to give your 15-year-old a hiding in the middle of the street? 'But he never has said anything like that, he's always done what he's told'. Always? He's down the street without permission, so you may have to face the possibility of a refusal to get into the car. What would you do?

Some will mention getting support from the police, who may oblige by trying to bluff the kid, but if he is not easily bluffed, bang goes another option. What would you do?

At this point most parents come to realise that they are back where they were when smacking didn't stop the 2-to-four-year-old and they have to find another way. They are back with the baby insisting on climbing the stairs, knowing he might fall and get hurt but helpless to do anything about it except be there to kiss it better

This is one of the forgotten lessons we learnt about raising children. There are times when they insist on learning from experience and we generally have to stand back and allow them to do it. This can be extremely difficult because some teenagers play dangerous games.

Other ways to discipline children

In Chapter 10 I stated that children will change behaviour if what they are doing doesn't get them what they want or ceases to get them what they want. In other words, kids only change their behaviour if their present behaviour causes them a problem.

When the kids were little you learned all these things and may have found it easy to do because you had physical, financial, emotional, psychological and social power over the child. You could, most of the time, control whether they got what they wanted and could deprive them of a privilege. Now that he's reached adolescence, most of this power over him is dwindling fast and passing over to the peer group, so you have to use another way to get what you want.

Let's have a look at another lesson you learned when the kids were little. Mum wants her child to behave and can't get what she wants by smacking him so she changes her behaviour to trying to bribe him with a lolly.

Hidden in this simple example are two principles of changing the way someone acts. First of all, we'll look at Mum's behaviour. Mum changed how she went about getting what she wanted because she couldn't get it the first way she tried. But if a smack continued to work for her, that's probably what she would continue to do.

Adults are just grown up children so what works to change Mum's behaviour will work to change a child's behaviour; if he doesn't get what he wants, and he still wants it, he'll have to change the way he tries to get it. But, just like Mum, he will continue to use the old way if it works in getting what he wants.

If Mum has control over whether he gets what he wants, she can simply say 'no' unless he acts in a way she approves of. (If grandmothers and others tell you how you should be doing it, tell them once what you are doing and why and then stick to it.)

There may be no problem with what the child wants but only in the way he is trying to get it.

The second principle in the example above is that changing what someone wants will change their behaviour. Mum influenced the child to want something else (the lolly) and the child changed his behaviour to get it.

It's far easier to change a person's behaviour when you have control over what they want, than it is to persuade them to change what they want.

There is no certainty that you will be able to talk her into wanting something else and you can't *make* her change what she wants.

Consequences

When we think of consequences we generally think of something unpleasant that happens; 'You will have to take the consequences.'; 'I had to suffer the consequences.'; but whenever we think of a good, or positive, consequence we generally refer to it as a reward; as a 'pay off'. The good result was our doing but the bad result was just bad luck.

Unfortunately, we tend to only notice the bad effects of a kid's behaviour and seldom point out the good consequences of their actions.

Consequences are not seen as an abuse but as something that rightly follows from the behaviour; that what happened was a direct result of the behaviour and if the behaviour had been different, the outcome would have been different.

The effect of a kid's behaviour on other people and things is one consequence but there has to be another consequence if unacceptable behaviour is going to alter. There has to be a consequence back onto the child and that consequence has to mean something to the child, it has to make his behaviour cause him a problem if he is going to change it. These are the reasons why a smack is so popular but a smack only happens when he gets caught. The ideal is for him to see that whatever effect his behaviour has on other people will come back on him in some way regardless of whether he gets caught or not. Sometimes it will be a quick consequence and sometimes it will be slow in coming.

Stage two adolescents will respond more to feedback about the social effects of behaviour from people who are important to them. Feedback could be what others will think of them, how it affects their looks and image, the keeping of friends, and how they are performing in whatever role they are playing at the time – as an employee, friend or sportsperson.

With stage one adolescents, it is still important to point out the social effects their behaviour is having even though they may only respond when the consequence for them is put in terms of the material cost to them or concrete things that they can see or directly experience. In other words, there would be a need for action to be taken, like the loss of co-operation in the form of privileges such as rides, favourite food, special treats, outings. Whatever those concrete things are, they must be things that are completely under the control of the parent and not things that can be defied.

Imposed consequences must be under the parent's control

When consequences have to be imposed on young children they are most effective if something about the consequence is under the control of the child.

For example, when he was little you may have sent him to his room 'until you decide to behave yourself'. Even though the child sees it as a punishment, when that sort of thing is done there is some control given back to the child.

If some control is given to the child he may make a connection between his behaviour and the effects. In this way he may see that a change in behaviour can bring about a change in living conditions. He rewards himself by coming out of the room as soon as he decides to behave. Most little kids will come out the first time and promptly misbehave again because they probably don't understand, or don't want to understand, but they eventually get the message, if sent straight back.

Teenagers are the same, they will agree to keep to the rules but within a short time may be back to disregarding them. It's inappropriate (and a bit difficult) to send a teenager to her room but you can adapt the principle behind it by putting distance between you in some way, by leaving the room yourself or other ways that will be discussed in Chapter 15.

Regardless of the age of the adolescent, imposing consequences that could be defied is putting a strain on the relationship unless there is an agreement about it and it is acknowledged that the young person could defy the consequence. For example, one of the favourite consequences for parents is to ground a child for being late home or going out without permission but all the kid has to do is walk straight out the door again. What are you going to do then? Extend his grounding?.

Grounding is a logical consequence, no doubt about that. The problem is that it is setting up a possible power struggle. The child is able to defy the grounding, by sneaking out the bedroom window or by openly going through the door and making it more definite by slamming it.

'He wouldn't be game. I'd soon stop that'. How? If someone wants to get out, they will get out. High security prisons don't stop people who are determined to escape and I doubt that you want to turn your home into a prison.

'This wouldn't have happened when I was a kid. We wouldn't be allowed to defy our parents or we'd really cop it'. That's no doubt true but that was just the way it was then. Parents, religion, and schools all ruled by fear and that was the accepted way of doing things.

Over the next two chapters we will look at what parents can do about misbehaviour. Remember, if the behaviour is affecting you don't ignore it until you really get upset, act early because the kids may have got used to the idea that you don't really mean it until you start swinging the wooden spoon.

The difference between punishments and consequences

Parents are being pressured to use discipline methods based on logical or social consequences and I have no doubt that these sort of consequences are far more effective than punishment in changing someone's behaviour. The problem is that quite often when I think I am imposing a social consequence, the young person is referring to it as a punishment. So which is it?

It would take a whole book just to talk about the difference between punishments and consequences because:

■ What one person sees as a punishment another sees as a consequence.

■ What is hurtful (punishing) when one person says it is not hurtful coming from someone else.

■ Social consequences can be seen as punishments by one person and not by another.

■ Even withholding co-operation can become punishing if carried too far or if it is too severe for what was done.

■ People can allow themselves to be punished and therefore it isn't really a violation of their rights.

A child annoys someone down the street and gets a fat lip as a result. Consequence or punishment? A kid acts out in the classroom and gets sent to the 'time out' room. Consequence or punishment? Someone steals a car, gets caught and goes to prison. Consequence or punishment?

We don't have the space to go into the nitty-gritty of all that and most readers would not be the least bit interested anyway, but it is necessary to give some sort of practical guide about this for everyday use.

As parents we can talk about logical consequences, social consequences and natural consequences and decide that we are using consequences instead of punishments but, in the long run, it doesn't matter what we think. The bottom line is that the kid is the one on the receiving end and if he sees it as a punishment, then it is a punishment. If he sees it as a consequence, it is a consequence.

The practical everyday guide is that the difference between punishments and consequences is in the eye of the one copping whatever it is and the judgement of whether it is a punishment or a consequence will depend largely on the child's knowledge of his rights.

When the kids were made aware of their rights they automatically became aware of when those rights were being violated. I don't believe there has been a rise in the amount of child abuse, kids have become much more aware of their rights, and the abuse of those rights, and are seeing some of the old discipline methods as the abuse of those rights.

Back when I told you about the rights of parents, you gained knowledge at the same time about when those rights were being abused. Parents have the same rights as kids, or kids have the same rights as parents, depending on which way you want to look at it.

One of your rights is the right to act assertively. Another is the right to not act assertively.

This means that when your rights are abused in some way you have the right to stand up for your rights and you have the right to decide to 'let it go'. But whatever you decide to do, you are giving your child an example of what to do when your rights are being abused and the example of what respect to have for the rights of others.

Sometimes you will over-react and sometimes you may let something go that you later feel resentful about letting go.

The same sort of thing happened to the kids when they discovered their rights. They became aware of the rights but many were not taught how to be assertive about their rights. Sure they were told to stand up for themselves but in many cases the missing bit was, 'while respecting the rights of others'. This is why your example is so important.

There may be many reasons why you decide to be assertive or to let it go; the value you have for the relationship with the other person; your level of self-confidence in standing up for yourself; what your friends will think; what the rest of the family will think.

Some kids who are punished are quite happy about it

Even though their 'rights' may be abused many kids are quite happy accepting penalties as consequences and don't see them as being punishment, in the sense which we are talking about punishments being a violation of rights. It can be said that they give their parents authority over them and are willing to accept punishments as part of that giving of authority.

As long as that giving of authority is from a base of knowing the rights and freely giving that authority, then it is not abuse. Other kids know their rights, respect and love their parents but will not accept any violation of their rights.

Kids who know their rights and give authority to others while accepting some violation of those rights are generally happy. They can accept and give insults as light-hearted banter with parents and friends whereas the same words from someone who hasn't been given that authority, will be seen as hurtful (punishing).

However, kids not knowing their rights and believing they deserve the punishment is not the same as someone knowing their rights and still giving someone the right to punish them.

It is easy enough to convince a person that they deserved the punishment. An extreme but common example of someone seeing a punishment as a consequence is a wife basher's victim who believes she was bashed because of the way she acted. She may really believe she deserved it and the man will no doubt say she 'asked' for it; that she made him do it.

This can be the long term effect of a child learning to use violence whenever he is frustrated in solving a problem, even when that problem is a wife he sees as being to blame for everything. The acceptable thing to do is to thump her. 'Doesn't everyone? Anyway, she asked for it.'

There is very little difference in principle between wife-bashing and the smacking of a child as a punishment. The smacking is seen by the parent as the result of the child's behaviour rather than as a choice made by the parent.

The child is responsible for the behaviour; the parent is responsible for the smack. The child may have been told so often that he is to blame for the smack that he shares the belief and sees the smack as a consequence.

'Well, if the child sees the smack as a consequence of his behaviour, and you say to use consequences instead of punishments, you have ruined your argument against smacking kids'. No, that is only an argument for better education about rights, to make sure every child knows their rights so no-one can fool them into accepting blame for the actions of others. Besides, all the other negative effects of punishment are still present, including teaching the child to use violence to solve problems, even when the child mistakenly sees the punishment as a natural consequence of his behaviour.

So it seems that the right to punish will be given if there is a sound relationship of mutual trust and respect or if the person doesn't know any different.

The latter should be taught their rights and given the opportunity to exercise those rights. They may not make distinctions between punishments and consequences as far as social things are concerned. Certainly they know about natural consequences such as fire burns you and water wets you, and you get dirty playing with mud. But everything seems to be imposed on them and they have no say in what the penalties are.

Kids who don't know their rights and who accept punishment because they think they have to will naturally try to avoid being caught and may develop the 'them and us' attitude to authority figures.

Some abuse of rights is 'natural'

The fat lip example given above would be child abuse and punishment if it came from a parent but both the kids involved probably saw it as a natural consequence of being 'a smart arse'. I don't condone the use of violence but it is a fact of life that some people do use it and if you know how a person usually reacts to a certain behaviour and you act that way, are you justified in complaining when it happens?

Another fact of life is that, as much as we would like to live in an ideal world of gender equality, there are different consequences for females than for males. For example, it is more dangerous for a female to be out walking after dark than a male so there has to be different limits, rules and guidelines of behaviour for males than females.

I agree that the female should be able to do all the things that a male can. I also believe that I should be able to drop a ten dollar note on the footpath, walk around the block and know that no-one will steal it. But the fact of life is that it will not be there when I return and I have to allow for what is, not act according to what I think it should be.

When a female dresses or acts in public in a way designed to attract sexual attention, it is a fact of life that there are male members of the public who will respond in a way she may not like. Is this the same as the above 'fat lip' example? I think it is; both should be held responsible for their behaviour.

This all means that there are people in the world, and there always will be, who don't respect the rights of others and some social consequences will reflect this.

'Fair go and safety' consequences

In the next chapter, we will look at effective consequences and how one of the great advantages of using consequences is that it puts the responsibility for behaviour back onto the child, at times causing the child to need your advice and support.

When we are using the 'fair go and safety' base for deciding on rules and limits we already have a built-in consequence system for those young people who are mature enough to respond on that level. The consequences of breaking rules and limits that were designed to give people safety and a fair go is that those people will not get a fair go or be safe and they will react accordingly back onto the person who broke the rule.

The child has to see the response of others as a direct result of their own behaviour for them to really see it as a consequence. If their behaviour in some way becomes a problem for themselves, they are more likely to genuinely change their ideas and behaviour.

This is because kids are torn between the need for freedom and the need for belonging. Freedom is important in satisfying their own needs but if that causes a relationship problem, they find they need to belong.

Things to think about

✔ If parents understand the meaning of punishment as 'the inflicting of physical, psychological, emotional, social, economical or spiritual pain' they may be more inclined to avoid using it as a disciplinary measure.

✔ Punishment prevents children learning the consequences of their behaviour.

✔ Punishment can do irreparable damage to that special relationship between parents and kids.

✔ Smacking may teach your child that violence is the thing to use when you want your own way.

✔ Consequences, as a method of discipline, are different to punishment.

✔ The 'fair go and safety' base for making rules has a built-in consequence system.

CHAPTER 13

Managing Difficult Behaviour

The bottom line for irresponsible teenagers

LET'S LOOK AT the bottom line first and then over these last three chapters try ways of not letting things get that far. The bottom line is that if someone is not sticking to the rules of a group, club, association, or whatever, that person is not welcome in that situation and is asked to leave or is removed.

Many parents have got to the situation where they have asked their teenager to leave the house and, if violence is involved, some have even taken out restraining orders to prevent the young person from approaching the house. Some have told the child, 'You are welcome to return whenever you want to but that must include being willing to stick to whatever rules we negotiate'.

There is no difference in principle here to when the teenager was little and you sent him away to his bedroom until he decided to behave himself. The big difference is that being sent away from the house, or being threatened with it, should only occur as a last resort.

Obviously, for the parent to get to the stage where a child who is loved for many years is being told to get out there must be a lot of the child's behaviour that the parent can't cope with.

In these chapters I'm going to look mainly at the behaviour of the child and almost, but not quite, ignore the fact that the parent plays a big part in the troubles by the way they react to the child's behaviour. I will assume that the parent hasn't yet developed the deep resentment that can precede telling a child to get out, the resentment that may prevent the parents from objectively setting fair rules and limits.

Alright, we have looked at the bottom line so now we will go back to trying to avoid getting to that point.

An overview of how to influence the behaviour of teenagers

Young people are trying to find out what they want from life and how they should act to get what they want in an increasingly competitive world. They don't have as many fixed beliefs and values as adults and their behaviour is their way of experimenting to find out what works for them and what doesn't. They will keep doing what gets them what they want and they are studying other people, especially the ones who are important to them, to see what is worthwhile having and how to get it. But should your kids follow your way of doing things if you are miserable doing things your way?

'Here we go, another go at parents about the example given to the kids'. You are dead right, that's exactly what I am going to do because it is so important to changing the behaviour of kids – to showing them what is worth having (values) and acceptable ways of getting it (beliefs).

Passing on beliefs and values to our kids

Kids are learning to be adults and they copy the adults who are important to them in the hope that, when they grow up, they will be just like the adults they admired.

When kids are little they copy the people who are most important to them and so are likely to grow up doing things the same way the parents do, including their way of being a parent. I heard a line once that seems appropriate here. 'No matter how hard you try to change them, your children will grow up to be just like you'.

Parents can be unhappy about the attitude of their children and wonder where they got the ideas they hold. Many parents are unhappy with the kids' behaviour even when it's obvious the kids are identifying with the parent and copying their beliefs and values. Maybe it's because there is a difference between what we say our values are and the way we act.

Some parents then try to force a change but today's children will not accept that. Values and beliefs that are forced on people may be the reason why so many people say one thing and do another, they don't really agree with the values and beliefs they are mouthing.

"HEY MUM..... WHY THE TEARS ? "

It doesn't matter what beliefs and values we intended our kids to see in us, the only thing that matters is the beliefs and values they do see in us. Maybe it is in looking at our kids that we learn a little about ourselves and we don't like what we see. It's always easier to see the faults in other people but not so easy to accept that they copied it from us.

Maybe what I need to do is to look at what I don't like about my child's beliefs, values, and behaviour and get rid of those things in myself so I no longer give that example.

Parents can be giving kids a double message when they are telling the kids they must change their behaviour. One message is saying, 'Don't do it', but the other message is saying, 'People are unhappy about the things you are doing now but those things will be the best memories for you later on'.

This second message is commonly given to the child when parents talk about their own escapades as children and obviously get so much enjoyment from the memory.

Adults get that 'far away', nostalgic look when talking about their misbehaviour as a child and tell kids how they used to do all sorts of things; how clever they were in avoiding the police, what they got away with and how their parents never suspected they drank. They talk about their misbehaviour as if it was the best part of their childhood and how much fun they got from beating their parents and the law.

'Alright, I agree that by example is the way to change what a child wants but we just argue all the time and he doesn't take any notice of me anyway'. First of all, back off! Hear him out without interruption, then insist on your right to be heard uninterrupted. Certainly give strong opinions but never argue.

Obviously, beliefs and values are passed on to kids in many ways, certainly not only by the parents. One young mother told me how she had carefully screened her three 3-year-old from anything to do with guns but he still went around the house using bits and pieces as guns.

There is no doubt in my mind that television and videos play a major part in the behaviour of kids. The people who make money from these things can present all the figures and statistics they like but those figures don't match the experience of people who work with children and see the effects first hand after the kids have watched martial arts movies, movies with obscene language, so called action movies, and movies that can only be described as violent.

The kids act out those movies, sometimes for days. The Kung-fu kick that just misses someone's face, the Karate chopping of the butter (well, you've got to start with something), the obscene language and general hyped up behaviour doesn't disappear just because someone says movies don't increase violent behaviour.

Try talking and explanation first

Make the young person aware of the problem their behaviour is causing by using 'I' statements that give them all the information they need; I feel . . . when . . . because . . . No blaming, no put downs, no demands. Just let the child know how their behaviour affects you and why. For example:

'I get angry when you don't put your dirty clothes in the laundry because I have to find them'.

'When the music is that loud I get annoyed because I can't concentrate to read'.

In most cases this is sufficient for a change in behaviour to occur because young people want to be accepted and to be well thought of. The older adolescent is very aware of being accepted and is sensitive to being put down or belittled so they appreciate adults being gentle with their self-esteem. They don't hold grudges and can teach adults a lot about forgiving other people.

The younger adolescent needs to be given all the information about how their behaviour is affecting other people so they move towards realising that how other people treat them is a direct result of their own behaviour. Don't argue with them about it, tell them once and let them think about it. Kids are not stupid, they'll nut it out but it will take longer if they are cemented into a position by arguments.

Attitude

Kids must come to hate the word 'attitude'. People use it too much, especially when they want a child to change in some way. Someone says, 'I don't like your attitude'. What the hell does that mean really?

Many people use the word attitude when they don't want to say what the real problem is or when they can't really identify the problem. They just have this vague idea that they don't like something about the other person, something about them is hard to cope with, so they put it down to 'a bad attitude'.

I tell kids to take no notice of the criticism of a person who says they have a bad attitude if that person can't identify a specific behaviour that is causing a problem.

Unfortunately, many people in authority keep telling kids they have a bad attitude and leave the kids feeling helpless to do anything about it. How can a kid work on something as vague as an attitude? To me my attitude is a part of me and because of this it seems very difficult to separate attitude from the person, therefore, if I have a bad attitude, I am a bad person.

Pointing out specific behaviours and the effects of those behaviours is far more likely to be effective than referring to vague things like 'a bad attitude'.

Stage one adolescents will not respond to talking, listening and explanation as positively as they will if they develop to stage two. Very often they respond with, 'I don't care', or sometimes, 'Don't tell me your troubles'. This is when action needs to be taken but because the emphasis should be on encouraging the child to develop an awareness of how their behaviour is affecting other people, the talking and explanation should come first.

A reminder about other points previously made

You want your child to act in a different way. Alright, let's review what has been said so far to get it clear as to exactly what is unacceptable. Question, is it the behaviour that is unacceptable or is it the purpose behind the behaviour? In other words, is it what the child wants that is unacceptable or is it how he is trying to get it that is unacceptable?

Remember to separate the behaviour from the person because that may be a big part of the problem. Maybe every time a behaviour is rejected as unacceptable the child feels rejected. If that's true, he will come to believe he is worthless and start acting that way.

Next, separate the problem from the person for the same reasons. The problem might be 'how to get better at maths' or, 'what to do about the breaking of rules'. It may be 'what to do with a drunken kid at two o'clock on a Sunday morning'.

Also remember to separate the rules from the person, particularly yourself, so that new ones can be made as long as the needs of everyone affected are taken into consideration.

While you are doing all this separating, separate the purpose or goal of the behaviour from both the behaviour and from the child but never separate the child from the responsibility for the behaviour.

Are her wants really listened to? She isn't likely to tell you her real plans if they get rubbished but she may be saying she wants things she doesn't really want. Therefore her behaviour will not match her words.

Exactly how is her behaviour affecting herself and other people in regard to 'safety' and 'a fair go'? Has this been explained to her?

Are you still allowing yourself to be controlled by doing the first thing you feel like doing? Do you still allow yourself to be sent on guilt trips?

Do you stand firm, say what you mean and mean what you say?

Co-operation

Previously I said that there are two main ways to change behaviour. All behaviour has a purpose, so to change that behaviour you have to either get him to change what he wants or prevent his present behaviour from getting him what he wants.

The fad of the 1990s is that a great deal of our behaviour and knowledge is actually inherited and the older I get the more I can see that this could well be true. However, inherited or learned, we still have the ability to look at ourselves and decide if what we think is important is really what we want.

When the kids were little, an effective way of changing what they wanted was allowing them to have a taste, if it wasn't harmful. Once they had it they didn't want it. This is difficult to do with teenagers because so much of what they want to do is risky.

Getting very sick from drinking may be the 'taste' at adolescence. I don't mean you should condone or approve of their drinking but when she is hanging over the fence emptying out is not the time to nag about the effects of over-drinking: she is well aware of them.

In an ideal world, kids would take heed of the lessons learned by the parents and avoid making the same mistakes. In the real world kids want to try it for themselves and learn from their own experience and it's a good thing they do or nothing much would change. Imagine Mr. Wright telling his two sons that he had tried to fly once and proved it can't be done.

When you used to offer a small child a play at the park to distract him from what he was doing, he had to decide whether the play was more inter-esting than the thing he was doing. If it was he would go, if it wasn't you may have offered to throw in a bag of lollies as well. What would you have done if he still refused? Pick him up and take him to the park yelling and kicking so he can see the good things there and want them?

With adolescents the idea is the same but the method is a little different. You can make information available to them about other things they could aim for, especially things that people they look up to are doing, or things that could be of greater benefit to them. For example, letting her know about courses available at TAFE colleges that some of her friends are doing. Maybe you could throw in the offer of an occasional party for her friends. Still refuses? Well, you can't drag her there but the government can by threatening to cut off her unemployment benefit, in the hope that once she is in the course she will want to be there.

Kids not getting what they want

You taught your small child manners by refusing to give him a biscuit unless he said 'please'. In other words, he didn't get what he wanted unless he acted in an acceptable way.

Another way of putting what you learned is, 'if a child wants something and can't get it one way, he will try another way'. When he acted in an accept-able way, you gave him what he wanted.

Teenagers know how to behave when they want something, they don't have to be told how to stay on the good side of someone when they want something from that person. Suddenly they know what to do and what's more important they want to act that way, because it gets them what they want.

This means that normally kids know how to please other people, all they really need is the right incentive and that incentive is that they don't get what they want unless they act in a responsible way.

You can arrange things so teenagers have to change their behaviour to get what they want, including approval and co-operation, and maybe they will discover that what they have to do to get it is not so painful after all and results in less hassle for them. They may even find that it works out better than the usual way they do things.

Using co-operation as a method of discipline

The real message a rebellious child is trying to get through to his parents is 'you can't make me do anything'. That is true and it is a right that they have but try to remember that you have the same rights and can say the same thing to the kids. Imagine saying to your teenager, 'And you can't make me do anything either'. Admitting that you can't make her do anything is only telling the child what she already knows but if things are to work OK and neither can make the other do anything, there is a need for co-operation.

Many people object to using co-operation as a consequence and I have many times come across the situation where a parent is quite willing to inflict physical pain on a child but is not prepared to be firm with them by withdrawing some co-operation. The same parent who emphasises every word with a smack – 'I (smack) told (smack) you (smack) not (smack) to (smack) do (smack) that (smack)' – may object to the use of co-operation as a consequence because 'I don't want to upset him'.

'Non-co-operation' is the most effective social consequence, it teaches co-operation, caring and sharing to children of all ages. It is also a natural consequence because co-operation, by definition, means at least two people working together to make life easier in getting what they want or need. If one stops, there is no co-operation.

Non-co-operation is also a logical consequence because if one person in an arrangement no longer keeps their side of the bargain, it's logical that the other person will stop putting in their share.

Many people working together to help each other get what they want in satisfying their needs is what a society is all about. This is why people gather together into towns and cities, because it is easier to get what you want if people share the load, care about each other's needs, and help each other to get what they want.

Two people working together can usually achieve more than they could if they worked separately and will certainly achieve more than they would if they were working against each other.

Getting the kids to do something in return for what the parents provide in the way of food and shelter is not always easy and is even harder if they have not been used to keeping things even by co-operation. Maybe it could be put to them that co-operation can be their way of being independent even though they are dependent on the parents.

An example may help me explain this concept. We depend on the paper to be delivered in time for breakfast, and yet we don't see ourselves as being dependent on the newsagent. This is because we even it up by paying the newsagent. For the newsagent to stay in business he depends on getting money out of us; in return for our money he delivers the paper. In this way we are inter-dependent, which is what we normally mean when we say 'independent'.

Some parents find out that trouble starts when the kids get an income from a job or social security and become resentful at having to pay for what they have always received free of charge. Young people may prefer to move out and pay big money in rent and services rather than pay for their keep at home. Don't try to make sense of it, treat it as a learning experience for both of you.

Parents don't give much thought to how much they do for the kids and therefore how much the kids take for granted. Parents have just always given to the kids because that was the duty of parents.

All that the parents may expect in return is that the kids show a little respect, do some small jobs around the house and go to school. Some parents make 'going to school' the way kids earn their general keep and pocket money and they are expected to share some of the housework simply because they helped make the mess. If the kids don't keep their side of the bargain, the parents don't feel obligated to keep up the supply of those goodies. Quite often the kids are more than willing to do their share but don't want to be treated like little kids about it.

Sharing may come hard for some young adolescents but the older teen-ager feels a strong natural urge to share. At times they may go to extremes in sharing things with their friends. What little they do have, they share.

Controlled co-operation

Controlling the level of co-operation is an effective way of controlling your parenting when the child's behaviour is affecting you directly but sometimes it is difficult to see how you can justify using it when the child's behaviour is affecting someone else.

For example, there is a rule of your house that no violence is to be used in solving problems and your daughter has thumped your son as the quickest way to get what she wants. You are using a consequences system and try to talk to her about how she can put things right with her brother. She refuses to even talk about it.

If you decide to use your co-operation as a consequence, it must be as a consequence of her refusing to keep to the system, not as a consequence of her thumping the boy. Your co-operation is tied to your need to maintain the system and as soon as she decides to either discuss putting things right or she actually puts things right, you resume co-operation.

The idea is to make it clear to her that your drop in co-operation is not a consequence of her thumping the boy but is a direct consequence of her endangering the whole idea of working things out on a 'fair go and safety' basis. Her use of violence still has to be put right.

The controlled use of co-operation becomes a powerful method of actively teaching a child the advantages of co-operation and the disadvantages of non-co-operation but remember that the over-use or too severe use of non-co-operation will be seen by the child as punishment, with its unwanted results.

A change in co-operation is what is noticed

There are two times when things really get noticed; when they first start and when they first stop. Sound is a good example of this effect, we notice a sound start but if it keeps up constantly we cease to be aware of it until it stops; we then notice that it has stopped.

Many years ago I worked in a factory and at first the noise of the machi-nery was so loud that I could only hear people who shouted but after a while

I no longer noticed the machinery and could hear people quite easily. The only time I noticed the noise was when it stopped.

It is a bit worrying that a foul smell can become unnoticed after a time but when it goes you suddenly become aware that the air is clear again. People in big cities are so used to their polluted air that they open a window to 'get a breath of fresh air'.

A sign to remind you to turn off the lights becomes so much a part of the scenery that you no longer notice it but would if someone took it down. Taste is similar too, when you give up taking sugar in coffee the new taste is bad until you get used to it and then you can tell if even a small amount of sugar is put in the coffee.

This is a very important point when it comes to influencing kids to be co-operative; either you have to start something new or stop doing something you are currently doing in order to get the attention and get a response.

For example, if you were to suddenly include a lolly in your young son's lunch box he would be delighted when he opened the box and think, 'Good ol' Mum, she isn't so bad after all'. Again the next day he would be surprised to find it there. After some days of the lolly being included he just expects it and may go off at Mum if she forgets to give him 'his' lolly.

Most parents do an enormous amount for their children and expect the children to notice and sometimes acknowledge their effort. However, to the kids it's just normal and no big deal. After all, 'That's what Mum has always done, it's just the way Mum is'. Mum complains about people taking her efforts for granted, and she's right, but the only one who can do anything about it is Mum; she can get attention and a response simply by altering what she is doing.

One of the problems with this is that Mum is happy doing what she's doing and wants to continue to provide for her family in the same old way. She simply wants her efforts to be appreciated. In an ideal world people would continue to appreciate her efforts but it is not a perfect world. Once people get used to being treated in a certain way they come to expect to be treated that way, as simply the normal way, and Mum would have to do better and better if she wants her efforts noticed.

If she decides to keep doing more and more, she eventually becomes a slave whose whole life is consumed in doing things for others and nothing for herself. But if she decides to step back a bit and stop doing something, she can use a stop-start method of maintaining the present level of service to her family and still have her efforts noticed.

Parents seem very reluctant to withdraw co-operation and many feel guilty about using it as a means of disciplining children. Some are tempted to use punishment to get the child to co-operate but this takes the child's attention off the actual effect of her behaviour and focuses on the power difference in the relationship. Parents who defend the use of punishment say they are teaching the kids to co-operate; I believe that in fact it teaches kids the opposite, to be competitive.

Co-operation or competition?

Some young people seem to want to take everything and give nothing in return. They break the rules, refuse to do their share, take more than they are entitled to, threaten others so they get more than their fair share, and are masters of the use of logical argument to get a better deal for themselves at the expense of others.

This could well be the result of so much emphasis being placed on competition instead of on co-operation. Kids may be told to share and care and help other people and yet the kids are also getting the stronger message that they are to be beating others and 'nobody wants a loser'.

'Are you a winner or a loser?' implies that there is only one or the other and only winners are worthwhile. So, the only way a person can be a winner and a worthwhile person is to be beating other people. Add the saying, 'All's fair in love and war', and they can beat people anyway they want. A person who wants to be co-operative, caring, and helpful is a wimp and how many kids want to known as a wimp?

'There is nothing wrong with good healthy competition', someone will say. That's right, but to a lot of people the meaning of 'good, healthy competition' is that winning is everything. The attitude of winning at all costs allows the use of violence and abuse to be excused under the heading of 'good healthy competition'.

I also believe in good healthy competition but the best competition is with myself, not between me and another person. How can you be in competition with yourself? Dead easy. Swimmers, track and field athletes, golfers and many others are now talking in terms of their 'PBs', their personal best. They are competing against their own scores or their own times in order to judge their progress and can feel good about themselves and their efforts even if they are not beating the scores and times of other people in the same sport.

It doesn't matter how that personal best compares to the personal best of other people, they can proudly talk about their performance in regard to their personal best and get encouragement to strive to improve it.

With that sort of attitude to their sport or towards life in general they can be happy for each other when they beat a personal best performance. They win every time they beat their own personal best and winning only depends on the amount of effort they want to put into improvement or the amount of time they want to devote to improvement of that particular aspect of their lives.

'That's fine for encouraging kids in the sports mentioned above but what about activities like football?' Obviously in football, where some players appear willing to maim each other getting possession of a bag of wind to kick between two sticks at the end of a field or paddock, there has to be a winner and a loser. However, for both the winning team and the losing team, there is still room for personal achievement and confidence building.

" BUT MUM — WITHOUT NEW 'NIKES', I'M JUST NOT COMPETITIVE WALKING TO SCHOOL WITH THE GUYS ! "

Areas such as personal fitness, the number of goals kicked from a set distance, the distance the ball can be kicked, the accuracy of the kicks and handballs can all be used as PBs. Even if a player is not improving there is room for encouragement in the fact that she is trying, or the number of practice sessions she attends.

To use football terms, the co-operative approach would expect the players to be playing the ball (problem) and not the man (person).

The same attitude of being in competition with yourself can be applied in all areas of life, even to 'being a responsible person'. Judging kids against others may only teach them to drag other people down so there isn't such a big gap. The further others can be dragged down the less I have to do to get to their level and if I am good enough at dragging people down I might even appear to be at a higher level than them and not have to do anything to improve myself.

On the other hand, if I enter into competition with myself and strive to beat myself in achieving levels of responsible behaviour, I am improving all the time and it doesn't matter how I compare to other people.

Working under this approach, a parent would encourage a child to be aware of the child's own performance, to look at her own behaviour and to be trying to find better, more effective ways to get what she wants.

Taking the 'competition with-others' viewpoint, if there are five people who are concerned with becoming very attractive, there can be only one who is the most attractive; there is only one winner and four losers. Taking the idea of each person being in competition with themselves, there can be five winners and no losers. All can be encouraged in their efforts and all can gain a sense of achievement.

More about self-esteem

It's amazing how much time we spend following ideas that don't work, and rubbishing other people as a way to boost our own self-esteem is one of them. Years ago, this faulty idea led us to put physically deformed people in sideshows so that 'normal' people could gawk at them like they would at animals in the zoo. (When I go to the Zoo, I wonder if the animals are looking at us as curiosities.)

This put down of other people comes about if we measure our self-esteem in relation to other people and the measure of our self-esteem can only be the difference between ourselves and another person. It therefore becomes important to most of us to put people down, or pull them down, to make us look taller in respect to them. The 'Tall Poppy Syndrome' is still very much alive and well.

A child's self-esteem has a lot to do with the judgment of performance. The self-esteem of young people is very delicate at any time and if they judge themselves in relation to someone else's performance, that self-esteem is always dependent on not being beaten at something. For most people, the self-esteem must take a beating because there is always someone better around.

Besides, the self-esteem would be going up and down if it is judged by the difference between people's abilities, because that difference keeps changing.

Self-esteem would be far more stable if it was judged by that person against their own performance in every aspect of life. In that way they would become more aware of their own behaviour and take more responsibility for that behaviour, knowing that it is by their own effort that they can improve their performance, at sport or in general responsible behaviour.

" HMM.. GOOD EXAMPLES OF LOW SELF-ESTEEM.... "

Things to think about

✔ Learn how to influence the child's behaviour before a crisis point occurs. in coping with that behaviour.

✔ Influencing a child's behaviour can be done through example, talking and explaining, and co-operation.

✔ Co-operation and non-co-operation can be used as disciplinary measures.

✔ Co-operation with others is more useful for achieving goals than competition with others.

✔ 'Personal best' competition makes every child a winner.

CHAPTER 14

Consequences

Freedom becomes important

THERE ARE SOME similarities between the teenage turmoil and rebellion and the turmoil and rebellion of the 2-year-olds but the teenage version is not as amusing because of the dangerous behaviours involved and the tendencies of teenagers to turn to the peer group for guidance.

Kids going through this stage of turmoil need gentle but very firm and clear guidelines. The difficulty is that their need for independence makes it harder to restrict them to what they are capable of handling than it was when they were two or three. Back then you could physically pick them up and put them in the secure back yard, but that might be a bit tricky to do at adolescence.

Rescuing children

The aim of parenting is to help a child become a responsible independent person. Initially this means teaching kids how to do things but once the child is able to do something for himself, why does the parent continue to do it for him?

Looking at it coldly, every time the parent does something for a child that the child is capable of doing, the parent is rescuing the child, and every time the parent rescues the child the parent is depriving the child of practice at being responsible and independent.

Example

When a kid's actions resulted in his unemployment benefit being cut off for a while, his parents gave him money because he said if they didn't he would steal what he wanted, which he said would be

their fault for being too mean to give him money. Although they
didn't even get a 'thankyou' in return, they couldn't or wouldn't
see that rescuing him, without some effort on his part to earn the
money, was helping him to be irresponsible.

I'm not saying that the parent should never rescue a child because you are
duty bound to rescue anyone who is in real danger. To allow anyone to come
to real harm when you are in a position to prevent that harm is irresponsible
and could even be criminal. Besides, rescuing is a parent's way of showing love
and concern.

What I am saying is that the parent should know when the child is being rescued so that the rescuing can be deliberate and to be for a purpose; to show love
and concern, not just to rescue out of habit or guilt about their role as a parent.

If a parent knows she is rescuing the child and decides to go ahead, fine.
That is her choice and maybe it is the result of the parent deciding to rescue
the child in that type of situation and not rescue in another type of situation.
However, if she is repeatedly rescuing the child in a particular type of situation, the child needs help and encouragement to become independent in those
situations so he is no longer in need of rescuing.

There are all sorts of situations in which children and people in general
deserve to be rescued. Rescue when you should but be aware of when you
are rescuing so you can stop rescuing when rescuing is inappropriate. Rescuing can be a valuable way to show people that you care about them and that
they are important enough for you to go out of your way to save them from
something.

Whenever a person is hurting badly from a death or some other great loss,
people naturally rescue them from all sorts of normal responsibilities that they
are well capable of carrying out but in that situation rescuing becomes important to show the person that people care.

However, try not to feel guilty about failing to rescue a child from harm
when the child refuses to be rescued. Parents believe they have a duty to automatically rescue their child. If they allow their children to come to any sort of
harm they think they are a failure and believe that other people will consider
them to be poor parents.

You may be right when you think that some people will say you are mean for allowing your child to take the consequences but if they are the victims of the child's behaviour those same people would probably condemn you for failing to discipline him.

Try not to be influenced by what you think people will say about your parenting, the important thing is that you do what you think is best in moving your children closer to becoming responsible independent people. That means teaching them how to act, allowing them to practise what you have shown them, encouraging their efforts and allowing them to find out for themselves how their efforts turned out.

Once you are sure your child knows a responsible way to do something, he should be encouraged to act responsibly and expected to act responsibly. Whether he decides to act responsibly or not is up to him and he has to be the one to experience the result of that decision. Rescuing someone who decides to act irresponsibly encourages irresponsible behaviour and as we saw in an earlier chapter, this leads to the destructive negative spiral.

Should you stop rescuing the kids? If everything is going along alright in the home, why disturb things by changing anything? But if there are problems with getting co-operation or a power struggle exists or you are left as the problem solver of the family, have a look at what others are capable of doing and ask yourself why you are still doing it. Many family problems are the result of parents rescuing the kids from doing things they are quite capable of doing themselves.

The 'problem solver'

Some parents are the 'problem solvers' and the whole family leave them with every problem to be solved. One parent will take this role, in a two parent family, and other family members will say, 'Anything Mum decides is alright with me, she's the main one affected so we just go along with whatever she decides'. What a load of hogwash. What really happens is that everyone can then do whatever they like, break whatever rule they want to break and when caught say, 'Well, I never did agree with that rule but I didn't want to go against Mum'.

Trying to introduce agreements to such a family is very difficult because no-one wants to make a commitment to an agreement. All members will continue to say, 'Whatever Mum wants, she's the one who makes the decisions'.

What they don't say is, 'And then if it doesn't work it's her fault', but that's generally what it means. Mum may even protect her decision making role by making all sorts of excuses why others can't be expected to make agreements.

Some problem solvers genuinely want to change the way their family is operating and genuinely want to find a way of changing things but they think they are in a 'no win' situation. If they don't make the decisions, the whole place seems to fall to bits and if they do make the decisions, everyone just lets them make them and nothing changes.

Maybe if she stood firm and let things fall to pieces for a while they would start solving a few problems for themselves.

Practical examples of consequences that put responsibility on the teenager

Some of the following examples were taken directly from our experience working with teenagers in residential care and some are taken from parents we have worked with. Some are examples of consequences that were negotiated, some were imposed because the child refused to negotiate, some are examples of putting the responsibility back on the teenager, and some are examples of combinations of these.

Only use them if you believe in them and feel comfortable using them, not just because they are in this book. Remember, you should take responsibility for whatever you decide to do. Be careful because even the use of co-operation can be seen as punishment if it is over-used or is an over-reaction.

Remember, the kids will probably want to change when their behaviour is no longer achieving their goals, of which belonging and freedom of choice are uppermost, but they must *want* to change, have the *ability* to do it another way and have the *opportunity* to do it another way.

When kids do something wrong parents may expect them to express regret or remorse, to say they are sorry, but kids are usually only sorry for being found out.

It is unreasonable for a child to be expected to feel real guilt about something unless that child has developed a sense of responsibility towards the welfare of other people and the young adolescent may not feel that responsibility. It isn't that there's something wrong with him, it's simply that he is a young adolescent and not yet at that stage of moral development.

Don't condemn him for it, encourage his feeling of belonging by pointing out the effect his behaviour is having on other people and how that affects the way they treat him. This is not a true guilt about 'doing wrong' but it is a step closer to it and is as much as could be reasonably expected from young teenagers.

A new way of looking at giving permission

When you are using co-operation and trying to put responsibility back onto the child you sometimes have to be very careful about how you say things. I mentioned in an earlier chapter that I would never tell a defiant child she was not to leave the house because of it being impossible to enforce but this doesn't only apply to kids going out.

'You do not have my permission' to do something is entirely different to telling him he is not to do it. Being told he is not to do something is an order and the attention is put on, 'You can't tell me what to do'. He can easily defy being told not to do it by simply doing it and feel justified in doing it. He has won, he knows he has won, and so do you. Telling him he hasn't got permission to do it is a statement, not an order. He may still do it but there is no victory, he can't force you to give permission so there was nothing to win and the responsibility for going against the parent's wishes rests on the young person.

Because they need outside control, kids will sometimes go to extremes in trying to get permission to leave home rather than take the responsibility on themselves for moving out.

Working out consequences

Example

A 14-year-old-boy had been given a new pair of jeans by two young people. The idea was for him to return them to the shop saying Mrs Jones had changed her mind and wanted a refund. He was to receive ten dollars for his effort and claimed he didn't know the kids had 'lifted' the jeans. However, he knew he was doing wrong because the kids told him if the shopkeeper decided to check up on the request, he was to get out fast, which he did.

The effect his behaviour had on himself and others was discussed and it was decided that the family was affected to a small extent in reputation, the shop-keeper was affected because he would have been buying back his own property, and the lady whose name he used was shaken up that someone would use her name to try to defraud the shop.

However, the main effect was on himself because he was known to the shop assistant through a pool competition they were both in at the local fun parlour, so when asked if he cared about what the people at the fun parlour thought of him he decided he did care and wanted to do something about it (his behaviour caused him a problem). Eventually he decided to face up to the shop-keeper, explained what had happened and asked the shopkeeper to apologise to Mrs Jones for him but he refused to name the others involved because of the risk of getting himself beaten up.

When he was asked afterwards how he felt about what he had done to make up for it he said he felt much better and really believed he had turned an irresponsible act into a bit of responsible behaviour.

Co-operation consequences

Going to school is part of the responsibility of the child, not the parent. The parent's part of the bargain is to make it as easy as possible by providing everything for the child to go to school. The child's part is go to school and do their best, so that the relationship is kept even. Some of the parents who don't expect their child to work for pocket money have 'going to school' as one of the ways the child retains her independence and equality. (Austudy applies this principle.)

The use of co-operation as a means of behaviour management can start at an early age as the following example demonstrates. I was looking after two of my grandchildren one night and they had left a mess in the bedroom which they refused to tidy up. The more I tried to get them to clean up, the more defiant they became and they seemed to be trying to find out how far they could go before I would smack them.

I certainly felt like taking the quick way out but suddenly the 3-year-old said, in her usual demanding way, 'Get me a drink!'. I said something to the effect that, 'You want a drink and I want the toys picked up. Seeing as I asked first, I think you should clean up before I get your drink'. They decided that was fair enough and put the toys away and I felt I had struck another blow toward teaching them the value of co-operation.

It's very difficult waiting for the opportunity to show the value of co-operation, no less so with a teenager than a small child. We want to teach the lesson immediately and want to impose a penalty.

Example 1

One mother refused to cook for her son until he did his turn at washing up. Another waited until next meal time and put the child's dirty plate from the last meal on the table and asked him if he wanted his food put on that plate or did he want to wash it first.

Example 2

A young person refused to help with the shopping. Instead of blowing her stack, Mother simply told him, 'I want you to do your share of the shopping or do something else to save me time so I can do it all'. When the young person still refused, she let him know she was annoyed and what she intended to do about it. 'I'm annoyed and disappointed you've decided not to do your share and you know I won't let you starve. However, until we come to some arrangement I will only buy the bare essentials for you. Let me know when you want to work things out'.

'But isn't that revenge?' Not if the mother had clearly told him what she intends to do and he makes a clear decision not to co-operate. It depends on its relevance and the way it's applied but basically it's saying something like, 'I want to do things for you but I don't want to feel used. You can decide how long this problem between us lasts.'

The important thing after saying what you intend to do is to follow through and stick to it. Weaken and the opportunity to gain co-operation is lost. If a child is not considering the needs of others then whatever the parent decides to do about limits must be within the power of the parent to enforce and the parent must be willing to enforce them. It's no good trying to use something that can be defied.

Teenagers can be put in charge of how long a co-operation consequence or co-operation trade off lasts. 'I'll speak to you when you decide to speak to me properly' is one example. 'You won't be getting a ride in the car until you clean it. How long that takes you is up to you and all the time you spend arguing about it could be spent washing the car.'

Parents used to do this sort of thing when the kids were little to teach them co-operation, and it worked. So why not do it now?

Example 3

One woman got tired of the kids just dropping their dirty clothes anywhere and told them they had to put the washing in the laundry basket or she would not wash them. They ignored her so she left their clothing on the floor and just kept kicking it into the corner. It became smelly and got ants in it, as well as one snail, before the kids ran out of clothes and decided to pick them up and put them in the basket. She did spray the ants but only because they would probably migrate into the cupboards and get to the food.

Example 4

A 15 year old had been verbally abusive to his mother for most of yesterday and wasn't talking to her today, he went out without a word and left a note for his mother on the fridge. It simply read, 'Pick me up from K-Mart at 5 o'clock'. She wrote on the bottom of his note, 'Sorry, I haven't got time' and left it there. (That one appealed to my sense of humour).

Time out and quiet time for young children

The idea behind 'time out' and 'quiet time' is to put distance between the parent and the child until the child decides to be more reasonable. With small kids this takes the form of, 'Go to your room' or something like, 'Sit over there quietly until you can control yourself for five minutes, then you can join in again'.

Sometimes the child will test you out by threatening to smash the room up if he isn't allowed out. So use an area where there isn't too much that can get damaged or one which contains things that you don't care much about getting damaged. This type of blackmail mustn't be allowed to work or you may be training a standover man of the future.

It is important to leave the child there until peace is restored. The child who can get the parent to come into the room before the 'peace' condition has been met has had a victory and learned a little more about how to control the parent.

Many parents keep calling out to the child, 'Have you decided to behave yet?' when he is still obviously bashing around and throwing things at the wall. Even deaf and blind Freddy knows the kid hasn't calmed down, the vibrations alone would tell him that.

You may have to hold the door shut but don't vary the conditions or keep asking him to stop: he knows the conditions and will stop when his actions are obviously not going to work, or when he gets hungry.

Example

One woman had a 13-year-old-child who was throwing tantrums and she maintained she wasn't going to make the same mistake with the next one, a 3-year-old. Yes, she did put her in time out but before the child had calmed down mother would open the door and say, 'Are you ready to come out now?'. The child would stop and be good for a little while before mother would again put her back into time out. Once she put up with the noise for 45 minutes before giving in and asking the child if she was finished. The child came out again but it wasn't because she had controlled herself, it was because her yelling had finally got the result it usually did, her release from the time out room.

This mother claimed that time out didn't work but time out wasn't the problem, she wasn't using it properly and was using it for everything.

Even very young children soon learn that parents are easily blackmailed by threats of 'trashing the joint'. Parents find it very difficult to resist going into the room when they hear a hole being put in a plaster wall or when things are being thrown around. However, when the child is fifteen and throwing dangerous tantrums, the parents realise that it would have been easier and quicker to fix a plaster wall or replace a few toys than it is now to stop tantrums at fifteen that should have been dealt with at two.

Time out is the most punishing thing that can happen to a child. It is isolation, being cut off, banished, rejected. It is the equivalent of solitary confinement, the most dreaded of punishments. To use the most dreaded of punishments for everything means there is nothing more effective to fall back on when the child becomes particularly difficult and not using it properly means that the most dreaded of punishments is useless.

Quiet time can be used when other things like suggesting another activity or showing disapproval or taking the forbidden thing off him or directing him on how to behave doesn't work.

Quiet time and time out for teenagers

The ways you handled the behaviour of smaller kids will still work with adolescents but those ways have to be altered a little. 'Time out' and 'quiet time' are still only to be used for extreme consequences because when they are overused they lose their effect.

At adolescence, the distance may have to happen by the parent being the one to leave the room telling the teenager to 'call me when you decide to speak to me properly'. Or maybe the parent will stay in the room and put distance between them by telling the teenager she is going to be ignored until she decides to co-operate.

Imagine a father telling an older teenager to 'Go to your room'. She doesn't argue but leaves the house. In one way she has complied by putting distance between her and her father and yet showed her independence and defiance by leaving the house.

The rule with putting distance between yourself and the kids is to always tell the kids what you are doing, why you are doing it and how they can bring it to an end.

Example

One mother was tired of the kids following her into rooms whenever she tried to put distance between them so she would go into the toilet, sit down, put her foot against the door and tell the kids she would come out when they had been quiet for three minutes.

Things that parents have used to put distance between them and the kids:

■ The parent leaves the room or the house
■ 'No speaks'
■ Ignoring the child no matter what is said or done
■ The use of politeness or maybe even super-politeness
■ Emotionless or 'off-hand' responses, maybe even humorously exaggerated with a toss of the head.

These are different to putting up barriers that can be destructive, such as giving orders. The separation can last just a few minutes, a few hours, or the length of time can be put under the control of the child – 'call me when you want to discuss it'.

Attention seeking, power struggles and revenge

Example

When an adolescent was attention seeking and really strutting her stuff, her mother asked her if she wanted a cuddle. This direct confronting of the purpose behind the behaviour may break the ice if done with a smile or it may bring a nasty reply, depending on the honesty of the child and how 'open' the game playing is between you.

Tit for tat or an eye for an eye methods are quite popular as consequences and may be OK for smaller kids but could start a revenge cycle or power struggle with older kids. If you do use this method, minimise the dangers by explaining why you are doing it and put the kids in control of how long you keep it up.

For example, a child plays loud music at night, so the parent plays loud music in the morning when the child wants to sleep in. This seems very close to being revenge and could spark a competition to see who can do the nastiest things to each other.

When you look like getting into a power struggle or revenge cycle, back off, but don't back down. There is nothing wrong with telling the young person you are backing off to avoid getting into a struggle or starting a revenge cycle. This tells the young person the relationship is too important to be wrecked over this problem.

Social consequences designed to be noticed

Some 'one-liners':

▦ Extra food no longer available when food is wasted
▦ Mother not cooking meal when people don't come home on time
▦ Serving up food on dirty plate when washing up not done
▦ Mother singing 'dirty' songs when unacceptable tapes have been played
▦ No beds made when child refuses to clean up room
▦ Cold food sitting on table when child comes home late
▦ Refusal to cook meal until dishes from last meal are washed
▦ No food in the house because no-one would help buy it
▦ No meal or a different meal served up to a person who didn't pay board
▦ No cooked meal for someone who didn't do share of housework
▦ No work, no rides
▦ No respect, no talk
▦ No work, no money
▦ No politeness, request denied.

Suggested consequences that teach something

Child may agree to:

▓ Find out the normal penalty for breaking the law she has broken
▓ Get the latest information on drugs when they are believed to be used
▓ Find out about fire prevention or join the Fire Brigade when he plays with fire
▓ Look up the correct meanings of socially unacceptable words
▓ Find out alternative words for socially unacceptable words
▓ Do a survey of friends to get their opinion of 'whatever'
▓ Find out the sort of discipline used by the parents of friends
▓ Find out from friends what sort of restrictions their parents put on them
▓ Put things right again
▓ Pay for any damage done or for any costs incurred
▓ Return the stolen goods
▓ Front up to the victim of her behaviour.

When consequences have to be imposed

There are times when the natural consequences of a person's behaviour are not enough or the child has to be shown that his behaviour is totally unacceptable and there has to be a social consequence to impress total disapproval. Someone significant to the child has to step in and make sure there is a consequence to the behaviour. A significant person is one the child sees as worth taking notice of, for whatever reason, and he is therefore willing to work out and agree to a consequence.

One example of this is when there has been an act of cruelty towards an animal. The animal is not able to defend itself or may even be dead as a result of the behaviour. Violence towards defenceless creatures, human or otherwise, cannot be tolerated and yet it is very difficult to know what to do about it.

There are ways to handle this that may teach the child something about responsibility and caring.

The offender could face up to the owner of the animal but if the offender is the owner of the animal this isn't a very bright idea. Assuming that the animal is dead, the child could have to bury it. He could be expected to use some of his money to buy a book on the proper treatment of animals. He could offer to do voluntary work for the local RSPCA.

If that is not possible, he could make a donation to the RSPCA, the amount being whatever is the average cost of saving an animal's life. He could be put in charge of properly caring for an animal (under supervision). He could have to find out the normal penalty for this type of behaviour if it was reported to the police.

The bottom line

Leaving home

Young adolescents need outside control and show this by looking for permission to do things, particularly big things. Leaving home is a very big move and a person who looks for outer control would need permission to do it. Maybe the child's actions in making life so miserable at home is to get permission from the parents to move out. Being told to leave is much the same as receiving permission to leave.

Too many parents act as if they are afraid their child will leave home and therefore give the child a ready-made weapon for emotional blackmail. His actions are saying, 'You have to do everything I want you to or I'll make your worst fears come true, I'll leave home. For as long as you think like that, I have you under my power and you will do what I want'.

When he was little you would have helped him pack his bag. Time for you to get tough and take control. Sure, you want him there but he has to want to be there.

Coming to the end of the line doesn't mean the end of the parent/child relationship, it really means the beginning of a different parent/child relationship. A relationship of mutual respect for the freedoms and rights of both: an assertive relationship.

Firstly make sure the child knows exactly what behaviours of his are unacceptable and why those behaviours are unacceptable. This is done in a way that stresses that he is separate from his behaviour, he is acceptable but he is doing something that is unacceptable. The problem for the parent is that the behaviour can't be removed without getting rid of him. He is the only one who can drop that unfair behaviour. You want him to stay but if he wants to live with you, he has to kick that behaviour out.

Always remember that when you are separating the behaviour from the person, you must not separate the person from the responsibility for the behaviour. He is the one who behaved in that way and he is the one who must be held responsible for the effects of that behaviour.

When setting the rules and limits in such a difficult situation, it's essential that those rules and limits can't be defied without the consequences being under the control of the parent or that they have a natural consequence. To set rules and limits that can be defied is just asking for trouble. For example, if you decide that there will be a time limit at night, he can break that time limit and what are you going to do? Ground him? He can just ignore the grounding and you're back to the old merry-go-round.

What you can set are your co-operation conditions. In other words, you can say what you are prepared to do for him, or give him, in regard to washing, ironing, cooking, driving, pocket money, reminders, type of food (favourite or adequate?), the time you wake him up in the morning, the amount of time you spend with him, what part of the house he is welcome in, anything at all that you can decide to do or not do, and what you expect in return.

Just what conditions you would set would depend on how you want your home to run but here is an example of a statement setting out some conditions.

"ARE YOU CALLING A REMOVALIST?"
"NO — AN INDUSTRIAL LAUNDRY!"

Example

'You are welcome to stay in this house if you agree to stick to these conditions. When you are going out, I expect you to let me know where you are going and when you will be home. The evening meal is between 6 p.m. and 7 p.m. and I expect that you will let me know two hours before meal times when you are not going to be home for a meal.

'I expect you to pay the agreed amount of board money on time and without any arguments. I also expect you to take responsibility for the behaviour of your friends when you bring them home; you know what is acceptable behaviour in this house and I expect you to have your friends act accordingly.

'When I ask you to turn your music down, I want you to turn your music down to the level you know I can tolerate.

'I will only wash clothes that are put in the laundry basket in the hallway and will expect you to put your own clothes away after they are washed. I want to have my sewing room as a room where I am not disturbed, so when I go in there it means I want to be left alone and you are not welcome to come in there.

'When you believe that you are willing to stick to agreements let me know and we will talk about what the rules will be from then on'.

Throughout that whole statement of conditions there is not one thing that the child can defy and there has not been a single order given, not once has he been told what to do. He can't defy an order that hasn't been given.

You only set out what you expect, or what you want to see happen, what you intend to do, or not to do. The child is left to make choices about what he does, whether he stays and accepts those conditions or moves out. He is put in charge of how long those conditions are to last and is told he could have a say in the future rules if he decided to stay, but whether he stayed or not was left up to him.

At every opportunity, it was stressed that he knew what was expected of him and that he is capable of acting responsibly if he wants to. There was not one put down or attachment of blame and no loss of dignity on either side.

Setting the areas of the house he is welcome to use and not welcome to use is similar to the permission to go out. You believe he can defy this and just go into the areas he is not welcome in? Yes and no. Yes, he can go into the room, but he can't force you to welcome him into those areas. This is an example of subtle ways of setting conditions that can't be defied. Again, it is going along with a fact of life, the fact that you cannot make anybody do anything. I can't, and wouldn't attempt to force a child to stay out of any area I have banned him from but there is no way he can force me to welcome him in that area, and that was the only thing that was said about it, 'You are not welcome to come in there'.

If he wants your co-operation he has to keep out of those areas or he will be completely ignored while he is in there.

Violent behaviour, especially towards weaker members of the household, causes concern in allowing a person to decide for themselves when it is time to leave. When someone who may do something drastic is involved my responsibility towards other people in the house would make it important for there to be a clear understanding that the police would be called if anyone is hurt or in real need of protection, and that charges will be laid for violence. But even in this example, it is the behaviour that is the problem, not the person. The threat to call the police must be carried out.

The responsibility for leaving or staying is put squarely on the shoulders of the young person and he is even put in charge of deciding when he wants to belong as a member of the household. The distinction must be made that he will always be a member of the family even when he is no longer a member of the household.

He may think that keeping to the conditions for just one day is enough and want discussions held to decide what the rules will be from then on. Those discussions must be held because that was what was said but nothing was said about automatically dropping all those conditions. One day's effort may only result in a small alteration and an agreement as to when the next discussion about rules will take place.

Avoid the following, which is taken as being kicked out: 'If you go out, don't bother coming back'. Parents see this as giving the child a clear choice for their decision. To the child, there is no choice because they intend to go out anyway and therefore cannot return. Others will have selective hearing and only hear the second half of the message, 'Don't come back'.

Some will confront the parent with what is being said, 'Are you telling me not to come back. Are you kicking me out because I want to go out with my friends?'

When kids who have left home return for a visit

The separation of the person from the behaviour can be used when a child who has left home returns for a visit or when he brings friends home. If he or his friends are doing things that are not allowed in your home, they can be told that they are welcome but they must leave those behaviours outside the front gate. As I have stressed many times, when you are separating the person from the behaviour there can be no separation of the person from the responsibility for the effect of the behaviour.

When the kids were little you probably sent their friends home as soon as they started to misbehave. There is no difference now. It's your house, you have the right to say what sort of behaviour you will tolerate in your home. The difference is that now the kids are much bigger and you can't physically push them out the door or take them by the arm and march them home to confront their parents.

There are things you can do though. Remember what was said early in this book: that all human behaviour is for a purpose and that purpose is to satisfy some need of our own, to get some pay-off for ourselves. This means that the kids return for something or their friends come around for something. Whatever that something is can be denied them if they are not going to behave themselves while they are in your home. If they want it badly enough they will soon behave themselves to get it. Nothing about people changes much, except their shape and size.

Once the child has left home, and there is no violence that leads to a restraining order, the child can be told:

'You are welcome to return anytime but your use of drugs, violence, weapons or offensive language is not welcome in this house. If you leave all that "out there", fine. What you do out there is your business and I won't interfere, you can answer to the law for that but I don't want it here. That goes for your friends as well; they either stick to those conditions or they are not welcome here'.

To do this you have to be prepared to ignore rumours of his 'outside' behaviour, forget about what other people might think and don't read the court reports in the paper; while he is under your roof and sticking to your conditions let him take responsibility for himself and just accept him as your son.

This is tough to do at first and even harder when he keeps taunting you about lousy parents who kick their kids out but when he has to take responsibility for his own behaviour you might find he will be asking for your opinion and advice. Sound like a pipe dream? Many parents have found they get along much better with the kids after they let the kids take responsibility for themselves.

Things to think about

✔ Teenagers' need for independence often runs ahead of their capacity to handle situations responsibly so clear and firm guidelines are required to ensure everyone in the family gets a 'fair go'.

✔ It is important for parents to recognize when they are 'rescuing' an adolescent from difficulties their independence has led them into, so they can rescue deliberately or deliberately allow their child to learn the consequences.

✔ Telling a child 'You do not have my permission' is preferable to telling a child not to do something if you want her behaviour to be responsible and co-operative.

✔ When imposing consequences on kids it is important to first tell them what you are doing, why you are doing it and how they bring this to an end.

✔ Separate the child from the behaviour but do not separate the child from the responsibility for the effect of that behaviour.

CHAPTER 15

Parenting is a Community
Responsibility

ONE OF THE things that has changed over the years, as far as parenting is concerned, is that many years ago a person's home was a haven from the world. Once inside the home the rest of the world was more or less shut out so the parents had control over what beliefs and values the kids learned at home.

Now, however, the world invades the home through video games, television, computers and the Information Superhighway with the opportunity for children to have access to a vast amount of information, including the world's violence and pornography, beamed right into the family living room, in living colour. The powers that be claim that they have to cater to the broader community and it is the parents' responsibility to monitor the kids' use of these things, but parents cannot possibly monitor everything available to children via these mediums at all times.

Parents cannot win because if they deny the kids access to these modern 'necessities' they invite comments about depriving the kids of something that is essential for their education.

There is a further problem that modern parents have when they try to discipline their children; the community has them under a spotlight and everyone is an expert on how the parents should have handled it. Some are saying parents should be harder on the kids and recommend taking the parents to court to face up for the misdeeds of their kids. Some are saying parents are too hard on the kids and keep the parents in constant fear of being reported for child abuse.

"WE TRY TO SHELTER JOANNA FROM HARMFUL OUTSIDE INFLUENCES."

Some public forces work against parents

Parents have many forces working against them in their attempts to raise their children and one of them comes from an unexpected direction. It comes from the very people parents should be able to trust, people who are genuinely concerned about the rights and the care of children. Many parents talk bitterly about the number of those people who are encouraging kids to leave home and who are whisking the kids away without the parents having the opportunity to know what the circumstances are, or what the parents are accused of doing wrong.

There are many kids being whisked away from very dangerous and damaging situations and these children should be whisked away as quickly as possible. However, once the child is safe, there is no justification for failing to let parents know what is happening and what, if anything, they are being accused of doing or not doing. It may well be that the parents have done enormous damage to the child, and the child must be protected from further damage by the parents, but there can be no justification for anyone adding to that damage by doing anything that worsens the relationship between the parent and the child.

Kids who leave home do so because they are not happy about something at home. As far as the child is concerned, there is a problem at home. The problem may be easily fixed if everyone concerned wants to find a solution, or it may be very difficult to fix because of abuse or things that cannot be changed. Broken homes, through divorce or other tragedy, are permanently broken and the children are the innocent victims of this modern type of child abuse: the abuse of their right to a stable family home.

Because I work with and see so many problems come from broken homes, at times it seems there can't be any stable homes out there but I know that isn't true. I also know that parents trying to cope with a broken home and unhappy kids need the support of the community, not ridicule, criticism and put downs. Their job is hard enough without having community attitudes making it worse.

Manipulation

Manipulation is an abuse of a person's willingness to co-operate because it takes advantage of trust and caring and is sometimes difficult to uncover.

Communication is the thing that destroys manipulation and children who use manipulation can only operate successfully if the people they are manipulating don't communicate well with each other. One of the tactics used is to keep parents from knowing exactly where their friends live or not remembering their phone number so the parents can't communicate with the parents of their friends.

Some examples may help.

Example 1

When she is really going to an all night booze party, the tactic of telling you she is staying at a girlfriend's home only works if you don't get in touch with the parent of the girl she says she is staying with.

Example 2

'Sally's mother says it's alright with her if it's alright with you', only works if you don't check with Sally's mother.

Example 3

'Nobody else's parents insist on driving their kids there and picking them up', would never work if parents talked to each other and discovered that the only reason they don't drive their kids there and pick them up is because the other kids are saying the same thing to their parents.

Talk to the parents of your child's friends. And get to know your children's friends and let them know what you think, not by laying down the law or moralising but simply letting them know what your views are. Simple, honest communication in a friendly, accepting, non-critical way can avoid most problems that could be caused by manipulation.

The most common response from children on this score is to attempt to send the parents on the familiar guilt trip, 'You don't trust me. If you trusted me you wouldn't have to check up'. Another way is to confuse you with the logic of, "How will you know I can be trusted if you don't give me the opportunity to be trusted?"

The honest reply to this could be, 'You're right, at the moment I don't feel I can trust you to go where you say you are going or to do what you say you are doing. If you want things to be different, what can you do to satisfy my need to know you are safe and not getting into situations too difficult to handle?' In other words, put it back onto her, she broke the trust and she is the one responsible for restoring it if she wants to be trusted.

Kids are not the only ones who use manipulation. Parents can be the ones who have taught the kids how. One example of this is when a parent uses the emotional blackmail of blaming her illnesses on the child's behaviour. How he didn't seem to care that she got sick every time he talked about leaving home.

Example

One woman claimed she became physically ill whenever her son did anything she didn't want him to do. His haircut could do this to her and when he went missing from school she had to 'have the doctor'.

When he wanted to leave home, the only place he could go without her becoming sick was to some sort of institution. It turned out that he had some income and a place to stay but she was not happy with the arrangement and wanted to dominate, as she had been doing all his life.

Parents need the co-operation of the community

One very simple example of community co-operation between families would be for those who are allowing a child to stay the night to make sure the parents know about it. Not by asking the young person if the parents gave permission but by getting in touch with the parents. If there is sufficient reason for the parents not to know then there is sufficient reason for the authorities to know where the kid is, if only in case he is reported as missing.

People tend to believe the kids when they say the parents gave permission for them to be away from home, possibly because it relieves them of the responsibility of contacting the parents, and the kids soon learn to manipulate members of the public to get what they want.

Parents used to rely on the support of the community through the laws the community made but now those laws no longer exist. Some parents have been taken by surprise as laws they became used to have changed or disappeared altogether; laws that were once used to keep kids off the streets and to protect them from 'being in moral danger' or 'being uncontrollable' are now gone. Some parents still believe there are laws that 'make' kids go to school; parents are surprised to learn that 'truant officers' no longer exist and the law has no effective way to force a child to go to school.

Children are now very aware that they cannot be forced to do anything and they are quite rightly taught this. One of the problems with the kids knowing this, however, is that it becomes very difficult to make laws that protect a child from their own irresponsible decisions. The law is geared to protect them from proven harm from other people and to protect the community from harm caused by the behaviour of the child but the child can be making all sorts of decisions that have harmful consequences for themselves and nothing can be done about it. An example may help to explain what I mean.

> ## Example
>
> A 13-year-old-child and her mother have been engaged in a power struggle about the rules of the home for some time. After a big row about which channel the TV is to be on, the child runs away. She moves in with a group of people, ranging in age from 16 to 21, who share a flat, and it is believed that the 21-year-old-male is having sex with her. It is also believed that she is being fed 'soft' drugs but she denies all of this and claims they are allowing her to stay there, and looking after her, without expecting anything in return. Her mother wants her to return home and is frantic about the situation her daughter has moved into.
>
> Appeals to the police and the child protection service prove fruitless because the child claims she is being well treated and is happy where she is. The police and the child protection service cannot prove that any law is being broken but they are not happy with the situation. They express their frustration and tell the mother that they can do nothing because if they force the child to return home she will most likely just run away again. They advise the mother that all she can do is leave her door open to the child and hope that she will decide to return home before too much harm is done.

Experience has shown that laws that try to force a child to remain at home when the child doesn't want to, don't work. This is partly because those laws rely on the child fearing what the law can do to them. Fine them or lock them up? These are the sort of laws that we have only recently, and quite rightly, abolished. Another way of doing it is to make the parents responsible and fine them or lock them up. But once the parents have done all that can be reasonably expected of them, and the child still refuses to stay home, it would be unjust to fine or jail the parents.

The present laws do not give parents the support they need to combat the influence of third parties and the politicians say it is too difficult to frame laws that could offer that support. However, I find it rather curious that when the parent loses guardianship of the child, the lawmakers seem to find it easy enough to frame laws giving plenty of support to the head of the government department that assumes guardianship rights.

Children need the protection of the law – that must be the priority – but parents also need the protection and support of the law by making outside individuals and agencies accountable for their actions in regard to influencing children. That protective support for parents in general should be at least as strong as that enjoyed by the government agent who is given guardianship rights by the courts.

It may be impossible to frame laws that can be effectively used to protect kids against their own decisions but it is possible to frame laws that require persons who go against the wishes of the parents to justify their decision that the parent is wrong. I believe the existence of such a law would discourage many of those who currently collude with children in making irresponsible, self destructive decisions.

People in government and non-government agencies who are held accountable to the public, or through the courts, for their work in protecting children can and do make mistakes in making decisions, but at least they are accountable for the decisions they make. The mere fact that their decisions get so much publicity at times is proof enough of that accountability and is the way it should be. Parents can be thankful that there is a system in place that highlights those mistakes and keeps the workers on their toes. Fear more those workers and members of the public who are not accountable, their effect is only seen by the families they have damaged before they move on to the next kid to 'save'.

Most teachers, counsellors, youth workers, church people, and other members of the public act responsibly in working with the kids but each will only be around in the child's life for a very short time. But there are a few who, with very little knowledge of the situation, seem to 'take over' the parenting role.

These people may feel obliged to protect a young person by arranging or providing accommodation away from home and not informing anyone. There is no doubt the safety of the child must be paramount in the first instance but once that is achieved they should be compelled to inform a child protection authority of the situation.

The law could also set standards of care that those people must provide, including some form of supervision, just as must currently be provided by authorised carers. Such laws would not solve all the problems but might make people a little more cautious when they know they must be accountable.

As I said before, most people would not deliberately work against families but there are those who would and are not accountable to anyone for deciding that a child is:

1 telling the truth, and

2 is able to responsibly make decisions that have long term consequences.

Parents are helpless to do anything about those who are inappropriately making guardianship-type decisions for their children.

A 'helper' or worker may point to instances where the young person demonstrated an ability to consider consequences of actions, to make a mature decision about those consequences and accept them as the result of what she did. They then assume that the child has the ability to make responsible decisions about everything and should be allowed to do so.

"... *IMAGINE HOW YOU'LL FEEL ABOUT IT TOMORROW?*"
"*FAIR GO MUM — I CAN'T THINK THAT FAR AHEAD!*"

That's fine, but there is something wrong and the 'something wrong' is that they are not taking into account the difficulty that many young people have with seeing far into the future with any reality. The kids will say, 'I'll be dead before I reach 21'. This isn't a premonition, it's more of an inability to visualise themselves past such an old age. What's the point of talking about consequences that go into the late twenties, it's too far away to imagine.

I came across one woman who was giving training talks to youth workers and she was openly saying that in the course of her work she would lie to the authorities and to the parents to conceal 13-year-old pregnant girls from them, and would urge the girls to lie about their age in order to obtain an abortion. Her words were in direct opposition to the philosophy of the agency she worked for, so presumably she would also lie to her employer about her work practices.

The deceptions involved and the idea of encouraging a child to lie made it difficult for me to believe that someone who claimed to have the best interests of the child at heart could have such an attitude. In talking with others who were present at the training session I found that the woman's attitude was apparently held by some other workers and the main reason given was (and I agree with this bit) that it is ultimately the woman's right to decide what should happen with and in her own body.

However, they also claimed that it is every female's right to make those decisions regardless of the age of the person. A further claim they made was that they don't make the decision for the child, the child makes that decision: they are merely protecting the child's right to make that decision. In this way they can deny they are making guardianship decisions, wash their hands of any blame and be proud of the fact that they have 'struck another blow for individual rights'.

People working with youth must be constantly aware that young people are even more situational than adults. This means that any decision they make now will depend so much on the vibes the worker is putting out. Given another situation with a different worker giving out different vibes and the decision of the child could be very different. Is it then a well informed, responsible decision made by the child or is it a decision based on the self-conscious, self-centred, situational, short term thinking stage that the young person is at, influenced mainly by the self-esteem needs of the present situation?

Confidentiality vs 'duty of care'

There are many kids who have discovered that the words 'abuse' and 'suicide' are magic words that open many doors and they have immense power over welfare workers and parents. When these words are used, the kids find it so easy to use workers against the parents because of the workers' dedication to 'confidentiality' and to protecting the child.

Confidentiality is important but it must be weighed up against a worker's duty of care to the child. And part of that duty of care is the long term need of the child to have a stronger relationship with the parents, even though the child's immediate want is for something else, or their present need is for safety.

Some workers and organisations are so obsessed with confidentiality that they carry it to ridiculous lengths, sometimes in spite of the harm that is being done to individuals and families.

Parents have to face the fact that there is a problem at home and that, generally, the people the child has approached are genuine in their intentions: they really care about the care and protection of children and the rights of children. Community workers have to face the fact that children are likely to lie about just about anything. Some young people will lie so much it becomes difficult for them to know what's real and what isn't and this unfortunately works against them when they do tell the truth. Mix this with the fact that many kids see workers as being an easy mark for a 'con' job and we have a recipe for manipulation of any worker who worships the sacred cow called 'confidentiality'.

I couldn't count how many times a kid has asked to speak to me in private to tell me a big secret that I mustn't tell anyone else. When they leave the room I hear them telling everyone in the house all about it.

Striking a balance between the need to believe a child who is disclosing abuse and knowing that children see the truth as instrumental in achieving their aims is no easy matter for anyone working with children. Therefore the worker's first obligation must be to ensure the safety of the child, but how this is done must be aimed at causing the least damage to the child's family and the child's relationship with that family. There needs to be much more discussion about confidentiality versus the duty of care in regard to young people.

Based on what the worker has been told, he/she may believe that the parent is the lowest of the low for what has happened but the only person who should be making guardianship decisions (decisions that affect the long term welfare of the child) is the parent of the child, or an appointed person who is accountable for making that decision.

Things to think about

✔ Communication between families can prevent teenagers manipulating parents to allow them to do things parents don't feel well informed or comfortable about.

✔ Some parents manipulate children in order to maintain dominance over them.

✔ The law is geared to protect children from proven harm from other people but not from harmful consequences of their own irresponsible decisions.

✔ More support for parents from the law and the community is necessary to help work out problems with their teenagers and avoid an irreparable breakdown in the relationship.

✔ Only the parent or a legally appointed person should be making long term guardianship decisions for the child.

"OH, WOW.. LOOK AT THE TIME .. I'D BETTER HEAD HOME .... IS THERE AN ALL-NIGHT FLORIST AROUND HERE ?"

Generally speaking, children are very forgiving of the faults of adults, especially their parents, and will make all sorts of excuses for them. Most kids have great tolerance; they try to understand the misbehaviour of parents but wish they would listen when they are spoken to and show a little more respect.

Index